DISTINGUISHED
WOMEN
WRITERS

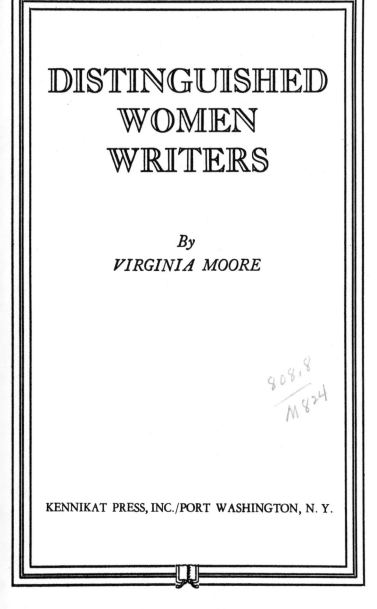

DISTINGUISHED WOMEN WRITERS

By
VIRGINIA MOORE

KENNIKAT PRESS, INC./PORT WASHINGTON, N. Y.

DISTINGUISHED WOMEN WRITERS

Copyright 1934 by E. P. Dutton & Co., Inc.
Renewal © 1962 by Virginia Moore
This edition published by arrangement with
E. P. Dutton & Co., Inc by Kennikat Press in 1968

Library of Congress Catalog Card No: 68-26245
Manufactured in the United States of America

Essay and General Literature Index Reprint Series

FOR
DR. JANNEY

Some of these essays first appeared in
The Bookman and *The Yale Review*

CONTENTS

o

CONTENTS—Continued

I

MARIE BASHKIRTSEFF

Iɴ ʟᴀᴛᴇ October, 1884, in Paris, a young girl lay dying. They drew the white wool *peignoir* closer but she could not get warm. The tasteful if ornate furniture was no longer clear to the grey eyes. She could not speak above a whisper. A figure which had been admired in Italy, Russia, Spain, and the most aristocratic *salons* of France, was sunk among pillows, but one could imagine its condition from the ravaged face. All was quiet now. What was there to say? Perhaps she remembered, as in a dream, ten years ago when at thirteen she had said,

"It appears to me that I have been placed in this world to be happy; make me happy, O my God!"

Did she suspect in the fantasms of delirium that this was the end? Tears ran down her cheeks, wetting the fine white wool.

Early in the morning of All Saints' Day they fastened a bunch of white flowers to a door in the rue Ampère, under an escutcheon with the initials M and B surmounting a coronet. When the white coffin went through the door there was a terrible cry. It was the mother, they said. A procession illuminated as for the funeral of a sovereign wound through the streets to the Russian church in the rue Daru. In the atelier Julian, a dark wreath was hung on the palette of Marie Bashkirtseff.

Many things pass in fifty years: many people of real and imaginary worth rise up and are laid away. Why is this young girl remembered?

She was not a great artist when she died, though she gave some promise of becoming one. Her beauty, however rare, has been matched and superseded; it has crumbled. There are only her few oil paintings, discoloured and flaking; a full-length statue in the museum at Nice, of a girl delicate and haughty; and the tomb at Passy. Her mother, her Romanoff aunt, her cousin Dina, her negro Chocolate, her servant Rosalie, all of whom adored her, have gone the way of all flesh. The men she troubled are at peace. Russia, her native country, has suffered a revolution; France, her adopted country, fought a great war. The ancient aristocracy to which she belonged has disintegrated, because the world has ceased to believe in it.

But an intimate diary of a hundred books was found in a white box. It begins:

"Of what use were pretense or affectation? Yes, it is evident that I have the desire, if not the hope, of living upon this earth by any means in my power. If I do not die young I hope to live as a great artist; but if I die young I intend to have my journal, which cannot fail to be interesting, published."

One thinks of other journals: Cellini's Autobiography, more famous than his salt cellar, Casanova's Memoirs, which keep him alive in lust and elegance, and the Confessions of St. Augustine, which do not conceal that he stole some pears. But are not incidents changed a little, transmuted, when remembered years after instead of immediately transcribed? Pepys' Diary was written from day to day, but Pepys at forty compared to Marie Bashkirtseff at twenty, in point of self-knowledge, was a child; their ages might have been reversed. Besides, Marie Bashkirtseff was a woman. That was the startling fact in 1884; and still is. Saint Teresa wrote a revelation of ecstatic religious experience; George Sand a frank autobiography; Dorothy Wordsworth a running account of Nature; Katherine Mansfield a literary notebook. But Marie Bashkirtseff's *Journal* exceeds them all in the strict, ferocious truth. And hers was the first.

All that she was, with its contradictions, is suggested in the *Journal*. Even in cloudy translation, the prose does not impede, it is a medium without resistance, like the sea to a fish or the air to a bird. Events—like her return to Russia, Walisky's death, Gambetta's funeral, a bull-fight in Madrid, an Embassy ball, the pathetic cutting of Bastien-Lepage's hair by his mother—are seen with the exact eyes of a painter, but three-dimensionally.

When she was ten her drawing professor asked her to copy some designs of Swiss *chalets,* but the windows were like trunks of trees, she said, and refused. At fourteen she decided that what most resembled Nature pleased her most. She loved the minute details of Velasquez, the very threads, with light on them, in the lace ruffs. This preference for reality was fundamental to her life—the backbone embedded in delicate tissue.

"Assume then," said Marie Bashkirtseff, "that I am of noble birth." She who had been born, in 1880, in Poltava in the Ukraine, never forgot it. Her father's father had been General Paul Gregorievitch Bashkirtseff of the Crimean War, brave, severe and savage; her mother's father was a Babanine of Tartar origin, whose family came into Russia with the first invasion. Both were provincial noblemen with vast holdings.

After two years of unsatisfactory married life Madame Bashkirtseff fled back to her parents. Marie's bizarre family now consisted of this ardent flighty mother, her doting grandparents, her generous widowed Aunt Sophie Romanoff, her cousin Dina, the daughter of a dissolute uncle, and an older brother, Paul. After a few years the grandmother died, and Madame Bashkirtseff's Slavic blood began to stir in her veins. Marie was ten years old when, in their wanderings, she first saw Vienna. A little later, at Baden-Baden, she says, she first felt the torture of vanity. For a while they stayed in a *pension* facing Mt. Blanc, in Geneva. Not till they reached Nice did they settle.

Her family seem to have considered it an honour to

submit to Marie's whims. Her dolls were kings and queens; she put flowers in her hair and played she was the great *danseuse* Pepita; and a gypsy told Madame Bashkirtseff that her son would be like everybody else but her daughter would be a star. At night the child recited this prayer:

"My God, grant that I may never have the small-pox; and that I may remain pretty; and that I may have a beautiful voice; and that I may be happily married. . ."

At twelve she fell in love with the Duke of Hamilton, whom she happened to see on the Promenade des Anglais. "He has the air of a king," she wrote in her journal, "and I know I shall be happy with my husband, for I shall not neglect myself . . ." When she read in a newspaper that the Duke was betrothed to a duchess, she was wild and inconsolable. "My God! Save me from despair! My God, pardon me my sins!" Plutarch, one of her favourite authors, had encouraged her to despise mediocrity, but had failed to teach her to bear disappointment with equanimity. She could not foresee the moment five years later when, in a fiacre on the Champs-Élysées, she passed the Duke, choleric and fat, with little mutton-chops, and felt nothing at all.

Like Juliette she was ripe at thirteen.

"The picture on the ceiling of the great *salon* of the Ducal Palace at Venice, by Paul Veronese, represents a tall Venus," she wrote, "blonde and fresh-coloured. I resemble that picture."

To look pretty she had only to plunge her face into cold water. Some said she was overdressed in her expensive Laferrière gowns, but what did it matter, she answered—if she dressed poorly they would only think up something else to gossip about. Who were these Russians? the society of Nice asked. It was rumoured that the Romanoff aunt had not come by her great wealth in the best way. Marie wrote with satisfaction, "I am very much noticed," and if eyes were hostile, "I could scarcely treat a king as my equal." On the promenade she drove a team of milk-white ponies with yellow harness. The cream cover had a monogrammed silver plaque, and the carriage was white, by Binder.

Her private apartments in the large villa were entered through an antechamber in red satin, with doors and windows painted Pompeian style. The chamber was sky-blue, and fastidiously kept; and from the satin ceiling hung a Sèvres luster; and the bed was shell-shaped. Her vast boudoir-study, with flowered cretonne, and woodwork lacquered white and rose, was studded with mirrors.

"I love to be alone before a mirror," she wrote, "and admire my hands so fine and white and faintly rosy in the palms. . . ."

But this gay, delicate and vain creature had the fierce intellectual conscience of a savant. At twelve she rebelled against vapid governesses and mapped out her own course of study: Russian, French, English, German, Italian, Greek and Latin, history, literature, science, music and drawing. A tardy teacher enraged her: "It is my whole life you rob in robbing me of my lesson!" At fourteen "after a day spent with seamstresses and dressmakers, in shopping, promenading and coquetting," she sat down in a white monk's robe to read her "good friend Plutarch," who cared, like herself, only for the great. When at sixteen she visited her father in Russia she packed, with thirty gowns, Plato, Dante, Ariosto, Shakespeare, some English novelists, and the Encyclopedia. She headed a letter with a quotation from Publius Syrus. Her erudition was the result of natural taste and a prodigious curiosity; and it was to be the means to her ambitious end. For she hoped all things, believed all things, demanded all things for herself.

"My soul is great," she said; and when, at sixteen, she was not a great singer, as planned, nor brilliantly married, nor the toast of Paris, she was not cast down. "My genius must be taken on trust," she insisted; "you have my word for it." Nor was her self-confidence without self-knowledge:

"It is my pride, my self-love, my complexion, my eyes, which weep and rejoice, but *I*, I reason coldly concerning these trifles, like Gulliver among the Lilliputians."

And she defended her eager desire for power, distinction and fame by saying,

"Happy are they who possess ambition—that noble passion: ambition seeks to appear well in the eyes of others."

She does not seem to have realized that sometimes ambition is noble, but not when it is a desire to appear, rather than to be, fine.

"If I had been born Princess of Bourbon like Madame de Longeville, if I had counts for servitors, kings for relations and friends, if since my first step in life I had met only bowed heads . . . if I had trodden only on heraldic devices, and slept only under regal canopies, and had had a succession of ancestors each one more glorious and haughty than the rest, it seems to me that I should be neither prouder nor more arrogant than I am. . . ."

But this ambition which was pride, and pride which was vanity, disarm by a strange humility, for while extolling her virtues, she stresses her faults. Young women who dare to tell the whole and absolute truth about themselves are rare.

She threw her entire being into whatever she was doing—flirting in Naples, impressing the amazed Russians, witnessing a bull-fight in Madrid, loving, despising. Honesty is a kind of energy. "I am consumed by inaction," she cried. And one day at Confession when the priest said, "You have committed some sins, no doubt; are you prone to pride?" she replied, "Very much so," but when he asked, "To idleness?" she replied, "Not at all."

Because of chronic laryngitis, her mezzo-soprano

voice, which M. Wartel, the most celebrated singing master in Paris, had praised highly, died in her throat. What now could make her famous? She had taken a few lessons in drawing and painting, and walked miles through Italian picture galleries, and at fourteen been critical enough to say,

"I don't like the Madonna della Sedia of Raphael. The colour is not natural, the expression that of a waiting-maid. Ah but there is a Magdalen of Titian which enchants me. Only—there is always an only—her wrists are too thick, and her hands too plump. They would be beautiful hands in a woman of fifty."

At seventeen, on her first day at the atelier Julian in Paris, she sketched a remarkable three-quarters head in ten minutes. Immediately she thought of the *Prix de Rome.*

"The question is," she wrote in her *Journal,* "to accomplish in one year the work of three. I am making rapid progress, so three years' work in one will be equal to six years' work of a person of ordinary ability."

Then she broke off. "I am talking like a fool. The question is not one of time." But she continued to act as if it were. M. Julian's students worked from eight till five, with a short time off for lunch, but Marie stayed after dark. Louise Breslau, a highly talented fellow-student, filled her with jealousy and desperation.

Three years passed, and she was not famous. It was incredible, but she was not. Bitterly she begrudged every hour lost in taking cures in watering places. Her throat was worse; she was becoming deaf; her cough was deep and dry and almost continuous.

Three more years. . . . She went to Spain and was revived, not by climate, but original Velasquezs and the Moorish beauty of Cordova, Seville, and Granada; and felt a dizzying influx of power. But the pictures painted on her return, at Nice, were only half-heartedly recommended by her masters Julian and Robert-Fleury. She comforted herself with plans for a great picture, conceived years before: the moment when Joseph of Arimathea has rolled away the stone, the people have departed and night is falling, and Mary Magdalen and the other Mary sit alone by the mouth of Jesus' sepulchre.

"What!" she cried in her increasing sickness, "shall my hand be unable to execute what my brain has imagined? Not so!"

Then the doctor told her, outright, that both lungs were affected, the right more seriously than the left; that, if she wanted to live, blisters must be applied to her chest and she must go south—be banished, she called it. She refused, saying that a burn would show when she wore a low-cut evening gown, and that she preferred Paris to any other place in the world.

Form in art, that was what she was really interested in, these days. Doctors were a nuisance. "A noble gesture, a beautiful attitude"—in a rush of enthusiasm she took up the study of sculpture.

22

But one day, resting from excessive work, she dreamed she saw a coffin on her bed and was told it held a young girl, and in the darkness glowed a phosphorescent light. The next day she was nervous, and drank a few drops of syrup of opium.

Her painting, "Jean and Jacques," two shabby boys of seven and four walking along a street holding hands, won a medal of honour at the 1883 *Salon*.

But what was a medal if she must die? But must she? She could not believe it. The desire to live at high pressure—faster, faster, faster—had seemed to warn of a short life. But she loved life on any terms and, in spite of an energy-sapping disease, had almost superhuman energy. "It would be cruel," she said, "to make me die when I am so easy to please.... I am sometimes sad, discouraged, enraged, but bored—never!" At sixteen she had spat blood, but X-rays were unknown in the seventies and eighties and consumption got a long start. Had it gotten a long start in her case?

At first her predictions of death were half pose; it seemed darkly romantic to be set apart from other people.

"It is impossible," she wrote at eighteen, "that I should live long. I am not constituted like other people; I have a great deal too much of some things in my character, too little of others, and a nature not fashioned to last."

Her lovely hands with bitten fingernails were genius marred by haste. She talked more and more about death, but still it seemed unreal, and she forbade her family and friends to speak of her as sick, and though often embarrassed, would not admit deafness. In spite of a heavy lassitude she kept on being furiously busy, and laughed and joked. In Spain, observing the thinness of her arms, she exclaimed, "Ah, this is the interesting period." But by February, 1884, she was more serious.

"I think I must be going to die soon for my whole life with all its stupid details rises before me."

She had said that she attended the Russian orthodox church solely to prevent people from calling her a Nihilist; but now she declared boldly that she could never believe in the childish God of the Bible, "only in the God of Philosophy, who in no way helps." In her childhood a broken mirror, or three candles lit in the same room, or a black cat, had seemed ominous. Now, on finding a bowl of tar under her bed, which her maid Rosalie had hidden there, to give her luck in health, she was so indignant that in her rage she broke a pane of glass. Bringing home a set of human bones from an anatomy class, she put them into a drawer of her dressing-table, and looking at them one night, mused, "In me too is concealed a skeleton."

But when she asked herself what was on the other side, immortality seemed to her more and more logical. "This transitory existence cannot be all; it does not satisfy our reason or our aspirations."

But she was never serious long; suddenly she would be again her old flippant self.

"The position of one condemned to death almost amuses me. It is an opportunity to pose, a new sensation; I hold a secret."

And,

"I came home so exhausted with fatigue that the sensation was delicious. Every overpowering feeling . . . is a joy. I remember once when I had hurt my finger . . . for half an hour the pain was so acute I took pleasure in it."

Could anything deepen this child? Could love?

It is curious that she called fancy, love, and when at last love came to her, friendship. The Duke of Hamilton had been succeeded in her imagination by Count Pietro Antonelli, a handsome young Roman and Cardinal's nephew, who had delighted her by choking his rival, at a ball, and by flipping, with a cane, a bouquet of flowers up to her balcony. She herself diagnosed the situation very well: "It is when I am tired and half-asleep that I think I love Pietro." He kissed her only once, but that was enough to make her repentant. Then, in succession, she flirted with, and took for granted, rakish Count Alexandre de Larderel of Naples, her faithful cousin Pacha in Russia, and the fiery and famous imperialist, Paul de Cassagnac. "To marry and have children," she scoffed, "any washwoman can do that." One married a rich and illustrious husband, she thought, for the sake of money, and position, and éclat.

Perhaps that was why she did not recognize Jules Bastien-Lepage when she saw him. He was not rich; he came from undistinguished though good stock; and was recommended only by his marvelous paintings, and by a pair of grey eyes "which had looked into the eyes of Joan of Arc." Still, she saw the eyes, and continued to see them in her imagination. How could their charm, she said, be appreciated by vulgar souls?

In July, 1884, Jules Bastien-Lepage returned from a hopeful trip to the warm climate of Algiers, not cured of a mysterious ailment. Chaperoned by her mother, Marie went almost every day to the rue Legendre and sat on the edge of his bed, and he turned his back on the others while they talked softly of art. She was twenty-four, but fancied her feeling purely maternal.

"I am proud, as if it conferred a new dignity upon me. He will recover from this, I am sure."

But he grew steadily worse, like herself.

She sent him milk from her white goat. Always exquisite in her person, she dressed for him excitedly in her diaphanous hats and dresses. He meant more to her, even, than the celebrated soirée at which she danced (against doctor's orders, and feverish) in a white mull Greuze gown, with garlands of Bengal roses. What was society now that Paris vied in praising her? To listen to polite talk, she said, was like being burned in a slow fire.

At the end of August she heard he was doomed with cancer of the stomach. "It is a new experience," she wrote in her *Journal,* "to see a man, a great painter— to see *him. . . .*" For the first time in her life she put another before herself. Dressing with difficulty she dragged to the Bois, to amuse him. Her *Journal* teems with his doings and sayings.

"That tyrant Bastien-Lepage insists on my taking care of myself; he wants to cure me of my cold, and buttons my jacket. . . ."

He suffered intensely. And Marie? She would be dead within the month but she was up at five o'clock, walking miles to find a painting subject of which he would approve. She made him a pillow with two of her handkerchiefs, and on it embroidered the letter J. In the Bois she played at preparing chocolate for him at the water side, and sat on the grass telling him stories. Because he liked her draped in a black shawl, she stood in a downpour of rain, with her hair coming out of curl, and would not go and dry herself. Her eyesight had begun to fail. But she took him for a drive; and at home put him to sleep by stroking his hair.

Then at last she could not go to him any more. But the dying man, with heroic simplicity of love, had himself brought to her, who was dying. Tenderly his brother Emile and her cousin Dina installed them side by side, in huge armchairs.

Marie Bashkirtseff, who in everything had dreamed

larger than life-size, did she forget the disappointment of not finishing her finely blocked-out "Holy Women before the Tomb" in seeing that head beside her—blonde hair, cut Breton style? Did she think of what the years to come might have held for both of them?

She was a mélange of lace, of silk, of plush, everything white, but different tones of white, and his eyes dilated with pleasure.

"Ah, if I could paint!" he said.
"And I! . . ."

II

MADAME DE SÉVIGNÉ

MADAME DE SÉVIGNÉ

I F Madame de Sévigné (1626-1696) could have foreseen her fame as a letter-writer she would have been amazed and troubled. The Comtesse de Grignan, yes; the mother praised again and again the inferior style of her daughter; herself, absurd.

But if fame would have seemed incredible to her, she is incredible to us, this woman of great virtue, but no prudery; of wisdom, but no ambition; of wit, but no vulgarity; of vivacity, but no coyness; of sharp intellect, but no wish to hurt; sun-loving always. We are troubled by the knowledge that such a heart, in just that delicate balance, will never be repeated. Was there no flaw? None, said Louis XIV, conceding her sincerity in an hypocritical age. Was she not insipid? Not at all. That was the miracle, and her most enviable triumph.

The mystery of character cannot be cleared up by a recital of ancestry, birth, and education; but a little light may be shed. Marie de Rabutin-Chantal, an orphaned heiress sprung from two eminent houses, was virtually adopted, at the age of ten, by her uncle, Christophe de Coulanges, the good Abbé de Livry, and was reared at the brilliant court of Richelieu and Louis XIII. There she began the studies which were to continue all her life. At eighteen she married Henri, Marquis de Sévigné, scion of an illustrious family of

Brittany, at the odd hour of two o'clock in the morning. From the start the handsome young husband took his wife for granted and was chronically and lightly faithless. But he seems to have been alone in his indifference, for, seven years later, at his death in a duel over a woman, her hand was contended for by the most elegant and eligible men of the court: Fouquet, the Chief-Controller, the Abbé Menage, the Chevalier de Méré, the Comte du Lude, the Prince de Conti.

She was pretty, if not beautiful, with an easy figure, silky fair hair, an "English" complexion, and bright limpid eyes. The "squarish nose" and "parti-coloured eyelids" may be discounted, for her cousin Comte de Bussy-Rabutin who mentioned them was angry at the moment, and when calm, called her lovely. At forty-six, when most women begin to wither, she was described as "shining," and at fifty-two as "handsome."

But the young widow was impervious to pursuit. Profoundly lonely for her philandering husband, who could philander no more, she quietly set about repairing her damaged fortune and educating her two children. "Nobody but yourself, in the whole kingdom," wrote her cousin de Bussy, "could bring a lover to be content with friendship." And, "I do not believe there is a person in the world more generally beloved than yourself."

But a human being of spirit must have a focus for the affections, and Madame de Sévigné's was her daughter, Françoise Marguerite. In power of maternal love she was like Cornelia, mother of the Gracchi. But no: her love should not be compared to anyone's: it was inviolable and unique, like every overwhelming emotion untainted by selfishness. But for the splendid letters, it would be mouldering with things past and forgotten: her proud sponsoring at Court of "the prettiest girl in France" would be forgotten; her assiduous search for a worthy son-in-law, though he would steal what she most prized; her terror for her daughter's safety at the birth of the first grandchild; her fortitude when her son-in-law the Comte de Grignan was ordered to Provençe as Lieutenant-Governor—all would be forgotten. "You are my only comfort," she wrote her daughter. "My dearest child, the only passion of my soul, the joy and anxiety of my life!"

The extravagance of this devotion verged perilously close to the abnormal. Her friends forgave it as the distraction of a noble nature. They pleased the mother, not by praising her, but her daughter. Nor was it all politic flattery. Madame de Grignan possessed, besides a sharp beauty, a philosophical mind; after enslaving a mother, she seems to have thoroughly charmed a husband. But, "Your little girl," wrote Madame de Sévigné, and does not appear to have considered it a fault in daughter or granddaughter, "pinches just as you used to do." "I love you so passionately that I hide a great part of my love," she told her daughter, "not to oppress you with it." And M. de Coulanges wrote to Madame de Grignan: "There is no such thing as talking to your lovely mother about you; large round drops roll from her eyes." Pale and feverish with hope, she waited for the post from Provençe; yet when Françoise Marguerite was the least indisposed, begged her not to bother about writing letters.

It has been said that Horace Walpole lived his life in order to write about it. Madame de Sévigné's life was not for the sake of letters, but her letters for the sake of life—a purer motive. At all hazards she must amuse her daughter, since that was the one way she could hold her. Before their momentous separation she had written a few unusual letters—like the delicious raillery to her cousin de Bussy, a masterful description of the famous trial of Fouquet, and the breathless "guessing letter" to M. de Coulanges:

". . . the most astonishing, the most surprising, the most marvelous, the most miraculous, the most magnificent, the most confounding, the most unheard of, the most singular, the most extraordinary, the most incredible, the most unforeseen, the greatest, the least, the rarest, the most common, the most public, the most private till today, . . . I cannot bring myself to tell you: guess what it is. I give you three times to do it in. What, not a word to throw at a dog? Well then, I find I must tell you. Monsieur de Lauzun is to be married next Sunday at the Louvre, to . . . pray guess to whom! I give you four times to do it in, I give

you six, I give you a hundred. . . . He is to be married next
Sunday, at the Louvre, with the King's leave, to Mademoiselle, Mademoiselle de . . . Mademoiselle . . . guess, pray
guess her name: he is to be married to . . ."

But when her daughter took up a residence of twenty
years at the Castle de Grignan in Provençe, she began
to write one, two, occasionally three letters a day, with
a rare and personal accent, and of inexhaustible interest. A tribute to Horace Walpole applies even more
felicitously to her: "An author who the least knows
what he is going to say, and the best what he says."
She rediscovered, after Pascal, the power of simplicity,
in times falsified by elaborate artifice. She could not
dissemble in living or in writing. "Mine is a blunt and
honest sort of love," she wrote. And, "Everything
unreasonable vexes me, and want of sincerity offends
me." She belonged to the group of *Précieuses,* and
her friends were the wits of the Rambouillet Mansion,
but in her soul she was a child. She was as solid as
Corneille, as exquisitely trustworthy as La Fontaine,
two of her admirations. Death itself, for her, had grace
because it was "no hypocrite." Her letters, using that
rational and magnificent instrument the French language for the generous purposes of the heart, are
models of style, encyclopedias of anecdote, mirrors of a
gay, naughty, gorgeous world, which they contradict
and refute. Yet it is doubtful whether they could have
been written in any but an age which put fascinating

conversation before cleanliness, before godliness even, among the virtues.

Everything which happened in Paris was material for this liveliest daily newspaper ever dispatched to the provinces. Ninon de Lenclos makes another remark, a gentleman is found dead on a street corner, war is declared, peace violated, the king's old favourite is jealous of the new, a strange style of hairdressing is invented at Court, a Princess is refused permission to marry a mere man, plague breaks out again, the Queen asks after Madame de Grignan's pregnancy. Her own quiet life is ransacked for details. At forty-five, a grey hair. She buys some rich stuff for a gown, lavender with shades of clear pale green, but will not line it with flame-colour as suggested because "it seems inconsistent that, when the outside is symbolic of frailty, the inside should express impenitence, indeed obduracy," and fixes on white taffeta. She quits Carnavalet Mansion in Paris for Livry and writing in the garden is "almost deafened by three or four nightingales." At her country estate, "The Rocks" in Brittany, ripe chestnuts are boiled, roasted, crammed into pockets, served up at table, trodden under foot. She reads *The Discovery of the Indies* by Christopher Columbus and is "diverted exceedingly." Everything is copy. M. de Turenne has the misfortune to be blown to pieces by a cannon-ball. The King, who composed a madrigal, betrays the Maréchal de Gramont into crying that the writer, whoever he is, is a fool. When M. de Guitaud's house burns he prances about naked but for shirt and drawers, near a lady in her under-petticoat and an ambassador in his frilled nightcap. The great Vatel, mâitre d' hôtel to the Prince, and distinguished for impeccable taste, whose abilities "are equal to the government of a state," this man, finding at eight o'clock in the morning that the fish for the King have not arrived, sets the hilt of his sword against the door and after several unsuccessful attempts runs himself through. Pomenars, on trial for his life against the Crown, is asked why he does not shave his long beard and says, "Who, I? I think I should be a great fool to give myself any trouble about my head, till I know to whom it belongs. . . ." Mademoiselle du Plessis boasts at table that at her brother's wedding they consumed in one day twelve hundred dishes, and when Madame de Sévigné questions politely, "repeats it twenty times, and will not take a single chicken from the lot."

Madame de Sévigné gave more love than she received, and knew it. The letters were her supplication. Though she wrote the Comte de Bussy, "Adieu: the desire to gossip has seized me, but I must not yield to it," for her daughter she yielded. A few critics have charged her with a tincture of slander. They are too zealous in their search for imperfection. She merely reported what she knew would be most welcome— the rumours of a dissolute Court. But, "I tell you nothing except the truth," she protests. "There is nothing I have greater aversion and contempt for than idle stories." And, "If I inflict wounds, I heal them." Apprehensive as a lover, she says, "Farewell, my darling: I finish, because I think I talk foolishly: and I must preserve my credit."

Her wisdom does not announce itself, is not forced. Fouquet "was irritated and therefore not quite master of himself." Of Madame de Richelieu she says, "An inquiry after truth does not distract the brain half so much as numberless compliments and nothings." Then her playfulness stops suddenly. "Love me; though we have turned the world into ridicule, it is natural, it is good." Her spirits are high, she is gentle and radiant, but when Madame de Grignan asks whether she is as fond of life as ever she replies,

"I find myself engaged in a scene of confusion and trouble: I am embarked in life without my own consent, and I know I must leave it again: that distracts me; for how shall I leave it? in what manner? by what door? at what time? in what disposition? . . . Shall I lose my senses? Am I to die by some sudden accident? How shall I stand with God? What shall I have to offer Him? Will fear and necessity make my peace with Him? Shall I have no other sentiment but that of fear? What have I to hope? Am I worthy of heaven? or have I deserved the torments of hell? Dreadful alternative! Alarming uncertainty! . . . I am frequently buried in thoughts of this nature, and then death appears so dreadful to me, that I hate life more for leading to it, than for all the thorns that strew its way."

And again,

"There is no real evil in life, except great pain; all the rest is imaginary, and depends on the light in which we view things. Other evils are curable either by time, moderation in our wishes, or strength of mind. But pain tyrannizes over both soul and body. Confidence in God may enable us to bear it with patience, and turn it to our advantage, but it will not diminish it."

So intense was her love for her daughter, and so blind, we are astonished by her cool and critical, though affectionate, appraisal of her only son. He is "a composition of oddities," whose

"sentiments are all just, and all false; all cold, and all warm; all deceitful, and all sincere; in short, it is his heart which should wear the cap."

Whatever Françoise did was all right, her least action, her most inconsiderable decision, was a proof of genius; but Charles, she thought, showed very bad judgment to marry at thirty-seven a girl from the provinces, Jeanne-Marguerite de Brehant de Mauron. During her lifetime and by bequest the mother gave much less to her son than her daughter. This doubtful justice must be interpreted in the light of an inordinate, and almost demented, allegiance.

With age she grew more religious, but not more orthodox, being a lukewarm Jansenist. Though free-will seemed logical, the responsibility of it oppressed. It suited her better to believe in a Providence which acted continually for a known or an unknown good. Superstitious she never was; Confession she did not take seriously; eternal torment struck her as a phantom of the morbid imagination. "I am not the devil's," she wrote, "because I fear God, and have at the bottom a principal of religion; then, on the other hand, I am not properly God's, because his law appears hard and irksome to me." Her private and uncanonical religion eschewed form, or indeed any outward protestation. Nothing could be more significant of her private criterion than these words to her daughter (though undeserved):

"I have long said that you were *true,* a commendation I am fond of. . . . Ah, how few are there of the really *true*! Consider the word a little, and you will like it."

Except for a growing anxiety about Françoise, she was as calm, steady, and cheerful in old age as in youth: a banterer with life. She had had griefs: the exile of Cardinal de Retz, a kinsman of her husband; the imprisonment of her friend Fouquet; Comte de Bussy's attack on her sincerity in his *Amours des Gaules,* delivered in pique; the death, inch by inch, of her esteemed aunt, Henriette de Coulanges, Marquise de La Trousse. But on the altar of her chapel she caused to be inscribed the almost heretical motto, *Soli Deo.* She had no abstract theories: only understanding of human values, and the graceful appropriate word. But in the beginning was the Word.

It is the wholeness of each letter which is most admirable in her vast correspondence. They do not grow by accretion, but are organic.

And that is what her life was. Madame de Coulanges said, when both were growing old. "It is a delightful thing to live with Madame de Sévigné."

She had everything at "The Rocks" except her daughter:

"my son, his wife, this pleasant habitation, company sometimes, books, conversation, walks. . . ." She adds, with her own peculiar mixture of sadness and good cheer, "All this will have passed, and a portion of life with it; which is a painful reflection for those who have lived long; but we must have fortitude, and make a merit of the impossibility of doing better."

She was at the Castle of Grignan in sunny Provençe when, at seventy, she contracted smallpox, that scourge of older times, and knew she must die of it. But with firmness she put from her the one thing she longed for with an intensity more than mortal. She would not allow her daughter in the room.

III

CHRISTINA ROSSETTI

CHRISTINA ROSSETTI

T AKE a fiery Italian temperament, transpose it to
Victorian England, convert it to the Anglican Church,
and dress it in black silk and a little tight cap. What
will happen? Something like the deathbed scene of
Christina Rossetti when she went into a howling
delirium and shouted at the top of her voice words
which her brother Michael could only characterize as
"painfully shocking."

"My heart then rose a rebel against light.'

Christina Georgina Rossetti was born in 1830,
incongruously in London, to Gabriel Rossetti, an exiled
Neapolitan political agitator, and a mother who had
been Signorina Polidori. Not for nothing was she
three-quarters Italian; not for nothing the olive skin,
the spacious intense brow of forty-five extant drawings,
the Latin cheek bones, the golden Latin eyes. The other
facts of her life and appearance are less relevant, because superimposed: the cold climate, the strict regime—
even, one might say, the thin correct mouth.

The childhood of this strange, pure, complaining and
powerful poet, what was it? She was not precocious
with books like her sister Maria Francesca, nor selfish
like Dante Gabriel, nor meek and shy like William
Michael. She was irritable, they said, and had a bad
temper; but this may have been rebellion against an

uncongenial environment. For the child was charming; everybody said so. She was pretty, and spoke Italian like a native, and loved animals. Every day she went to see if a certain wild strawberry on a hedgerow bank was growing—when not reading Keats and *Arabian Nights*. Then in sleep she dreamed that a wave of yellow light swept over the sky, a great flock of canaries sorrowfully going back to captivity.

And once while visiting her grandfather Polidori at Holmer Green, Buckinghamshire, she found a dead mouse, and buried it, and several days later removed the green moss, to look. When a big shiny black beetle emerged, she fled in horror, and—says her diary—never went back.

But all her life she went back to look at her dead mouse, and a beetle emerged, and she fled screaming. Since a morbid mind affects the body, she was constantly under doctors' care: for heart trouble, for a cough which threatened consumption, for a disease of the eyes, for a sense of suffocation, and finally for the cancer which in her sixty-fourth year proved fatal. Her brother Gabriel presumably did not know the story of the dead mouse and the beetle, but he referred in a letter to the morbid "skeletons in Christina's various closets."

The Rossettis were affectionate, proud and poor. The father's meagre income from teaching and writing was supplemented by Maria as a governess, Michael as a clerk in the Excise, and Christina and her mother as keepers of a day-school. Gabriel, who had a theory of the "necessary selfishness of an artist," contributed to the family, not money, but the Pre-Raphaelites: Burne-Jones, Watts-Dunton, Coventry Patmore, William Morris, Richard Garnett, Edmund Gosse, William Shields. In the Rossetti house there were talk and counter-talk, artistic, literary and political, for Christina to sharpen her wits on and broaden her outlook with.

But already she had prejudices. Science and history she would not read. Philosophy, except Plato, certainly not. Shakespeare, yes—but Sir Toby Belch, Falconbridge and Falstaff repelled her. Scott and Dickens, with misgivings. There remained St. Augustine's *Confessions,* the *Imitation of Christ* by Thomas à Kempis, *Pilgrim's Progress,* Homer in translation, Dante in the original, Shelley expurgated, Coleridge, Tennyson, her friend Swinburne, and—fantastically—Augusta Webster. At twenty she knew the Bible from Genesis through Revelation accurately, emotionally, as a child knows nursery rhymes.

Religion to her was a hairshirt. She eschewed the theatre, not because plays were evil, but because the moral tone of actors and actresses was notoriously lax. She gave up chess which she enjoyed, because "too eager to win;" took Communion on Thursdays and Sundays, performed oblations, prayed like Daniel three times a day, fasted, and confessed. She said she was not worthy enough to join the Anglican Sisterhood of All Saints with Maria. Had not Maria refused to enter the Mummy Room of the British Museum lest the Resurrection take place and "those solemn corpses turn into a sight for sight-seers"? But Christina more than Maria belonged to that unworldly race of fanatics, saints, dire prophets, and pure mystics who subsist alternately on faith and fear; and she had to take it out on her worsted, which knotted, and in writing pious verse.

See her through the eyes of James Collinson, the Pre-Raphaelite artist who loved her; study the chaste pensive Virgin in Dante Gabriel Rossetti's "The Annunciation" in the London National Gallery; notice the figure slender as a candle, the hands frail and shapely.

In a rich voice she inquired Mr. Collinson's religion. Roman Catholic, he said, converted from the Church of England. In that case, she said, she could not consider his proposal. Then Collinson found that, after all, his views were not incompatible with the Church of England; and so was accepted. Later his conscience pricked him and he must at all hazards re-become a Roman Catholic. The engagement was cancelled. But when she met him in the street one day, arm in arm with Michael, she fainted.

Ten years later—desolate years—she met Charles Bagot Cayley, a scholar who had once studied Italian under her father. After a visit to Gabriel's studio Madox Brown made this record:

"Heat intense and lots of strawberries. I forgot Cayley who looks mad and is always in a rumpled shirt, without collar, and an old tail coat."

One of his gifts to Christina was a sea mouse preserved in alcohol!

This man she loved "deeply and permanently," but refused him too. Though reared in the Church of England he could not agree that Christianity is on a different plane than other ancient faiths. Her brother Michael, now married, urged that if lack of money embarrassed, they should share his home. But till Cayley's death in 1883, Christina would grant no more than friendship. In that year she wrote,

"Very likely there was a moment, and no wonder, when those who loved you best thought very severely of me, and indeed I deserved severity at my own hands—I never seemed to get much at yours."

Does this mean that once she had encouraged his suit?

Replying to his premonition of death she had said, "Some trifle that you . . . had used would be precious to me." He had decided on his desk, in which lay a ring; and had bequeathed to her any and all royalties accruing from his books. The day after he died in sleep of heart failure his sister asked Christina if she would like a packet of her letters returned. The answer was no— destroy them.

Silently she took up the ravelled skein of her life; silently touched with her fingers his little volume of verse, *Psyche's Interlude;* silently, in arrested motion, stood thinking of his "gentleness and harmless manners." Michael, who outlived Christina, said that she was "extremely reticent in all matters in which her affections were deeply engaged" and he was "ignorant of several details important to a close understanding."

What was the real reason Christina Rossetti did not marry? Because she worshipped her mother? She might have taken her mother with her. Because of religious differences with the two men she successively loved? If Collinson and Cayley had been Anglicans as devout as Job, there is cause to suspect that she would have invented some other evasion. She was by temperament and choice a virgin and a martyr. It flattered her to be desired, for she was a woman. But marriage was another matter.

And within that spring of fastidiousness was another spring—fear—which lay at the root of her character. Whether fear was born in her, or bred, does not change the fact. But fear of what? She was sheltered by her family; with the publication of her first poem, at eighteen, she was a successful poet. "Yet am I wracked with fear," she said—fear of losing the safety of her mother, fear of "treacherous dialectic," fear lest pleasure be frivolity, fear of abundance lest it be unreadiness to "sell all thou hast," and, above all, fear of the unknown. Marriage was an unknown.

How could she be in love with an earthly man, when

she was in love with Christ? By Him she would be completely and richly recompensed for the abstinences which, in any case, she preferred.

> Many thrive on frugal fare
> Who would perish of excess.

Thus spinsterhood was not a sacrifice, though she tried to believe it was. She simply had to have a cross to carry around. Every giving-up, whether of chess or Cayley or something else, was supposed to raise her in the eyes of Christ, Who loved her reciprocally and ardently. In "Marvel of Marvels," magnificent apostrophe in one sonorous rhyme, she is one who, "precious more than seven times molten gold,"

> in darkness and cold
> Trembles for the midnight cry, the rapture,
> the tale untold,
> "The Bridegroom cometh, cometh, His Bride to
> enfold."

"For lo," she says,

> the Bridegroom fetcheth home the Bride;
> His hands are hands she knows, she knows His side.

Could Collinson or Cayley, estimable men, compete with this Rival?

Though theoretically death meant "Thine arms at last," is it a great wonder that when her prepared-for end approached she grew "painfully despondent" and had "an awful sense of unworthiness, shadowed by an awful uncertainty"? Is it a surprise that her subconscious broke loose in fury? Was it not inevitable that passion should take vengeance on the puritanic? She managed inarticulately to pray; and left a ring from her dead finger to the offertory of Christ Church; and the final dying of one who had been dying for years was accomplished.

Her preoccupation with death was not, as Alice Meynell has suggested, the practise of "an ancient discipline." It was the interned mouse, it was the atrocious beetle. "The heart knoweth its own bitterness."

Just as she liked to be horrified, she liked to be destitute and forlorn. At seventeen, before she had had a love, she was lamenting his loss.

> Would I could die and be at peace—
>   Or living could forget!
> My grief nor grows nor doth decrease
>   But ever is . . .

In the end, of course, she set a value on suffering.

> Pain is not pleasure
>   If we know
> It heaps up treasure—
>   Even so!
> Turn, transfigured Pain,
> Sweetheart, turn again,
> For fair thou art as moonrise after rain.

Paradoxically, she wrote *Sing-Song,* a charming

book of verse for children, yet did not care for children.
She was continually dosing and summoning doctors, yet
outlived all of her family except Michael. She loved
Nature, yet stayed close indoors. She had a delightful
sense of humour, yet quibbled sombrely over trivialities.
Of her own free will she rejected her lover, yet in her
fifty-second year wrote *"Monna Innominata,"* a
sequence of love sonnets unsurpassed in their *genre,*
tortured and beautiful. One of them admits her contradictory nature:

> Trust me, I have not earned your dear rebuke,—
> I love, as you would have me, God the most;
> Must lose not Him, but you, must one be lost;
> Nor with Lot's wife cast back a faithless look,
> Unready to forego what I forsook;
> This say I, having counted up the cost,
> This, though I be the feeblest of God's host,
> The sorriest sheep Christ shepherds with His crook.
> Yet while I love my God the most, I deem
> That I can never love you overmuch;
> I love Him more, so let me love you too;
> Yea, as I apprehend it, love is such
> I cannot love you if I love not Him,
> I cannot love Him if I love not you.

She tries to disown the contradiction:

> But by my heart of love laid bare to you,
> My love that you can make not void nor vain,
> Love that foregoes you but to claim anew
> Beyond this passage of the gate of death,
> I charge you at the Judgment make it plain
> My love for you was life and not a breath.

Then, though marriage had been refused from within, she pretends to herself it has been frustrated from without.

> Thinking of you, and all that was, and all
> That might have been and now can never be,
> I feel your honoured excellence, and see
> Myself unworthy of the happier call . . .

She was like King David dancing before the Ark and crying, "I will yet be more vile than thus, and will be base in mine own sight."

In these later years an affliction made her lovely eyes almost start from their sockets and sadly altered the colour of her skin. A bow of lavender ribbon held the narrow frill at her throat, and a long gold watch-chain fell to her lap.

> Part of my life is dead, part sick, and part
> Is all on fire within.

But there *was* fire. There were visions of immensity wherein old symbols, deadened by orthodoxy, leaped into newness of life—like "The Convent Threshold," the history of a soul which deliberately renounces earthly love to gain the love of heaven, but does not renounce it forever:

> Therefore in patience I possess my soul;
> Yea, therefore as a flint I set my face,
> To pluck down, to build up again the whole—
> But in a distant place.

"Il Roseggiar Dell' Oriente," twenty-one Italian poems written just after she had rejected Cayley, and candid in a different way than *"Monna Innominata,"* were found in her desk at death. In the privacy of another language she could admit that in spite of aversion to the intimacies of marriage, and distrust of instinct, in spite of her espousal to Christ, she had a normal human wish for a home.

> Would we were together
> In the beautiful spring weather;
> Who would care a feather
> Where we feathered our nest?
> That place would be like heaven,—
> Ah, would the gift were given,
> For I am sorely driven
> And you are unpossessed. . . .

In heaven she claimed him—and the right to reform him.

> Your recompense will be the one
> That you implored,
> And your enfranchised soul will be
> My full reward.

As if to avoid being guilty of the crime of consistency, her gloom, which seems so deeply established, is broken now and again by gayety and hope. She who called herself

> alike unfit
> For healthy joy and salutary pain

could see, like Whitman, that

"All suffices reckoned rightly."

At her happiest she could write "A Birthday," which soars so delightfully, and

> Heaven overarches you and me,
> And all earth's gardens and her graves.
> Look up with me, until we see
> The day break and the shadows flee.
> What though tonight wrecks you and me
> If so tomorrow saves. . . .

No good poet has been read more superficially than Christina Rossetti. Readers are intimidated by the size and bulk of her *Poetical Works,* half of which is mediocre, and only half distinguished in quality. The impatient judge her by requoted anthology pieces, such as "Passing Away," "Goblin Market," and "Remember," being ignorant of poems as fine or finer, like "The Bourne," "Three Stages," "Who Shall Deliver Me?" "Up Hill," "Autumn Violets," and "From House to Home." It is unfortunate that her work was not pruned at publication. But this was not the fault of the poet, who was meticulous in self-criticism, but of her brother Michael, who, without authority for the presumption, printed every scrap he could find after her death.

For forty years (she died in 1894) her ability waxed and waned very little: it simply was. Her technical innovations were fortuitous. Alive or dull, the poems

all but wrote themselves. At best they are clear as
spring water which, in unexpected places, bubbles to
the surface. They are simple statements of all but
fathomless emotion, in the tone of voice of one so close
to the judgment day when all will be told that candour
gains nothing, loses nothing, but is a kind of peace.
This directness is in contrast to the circuitousness
usually, and rightly, attributed to women. Reticent and
stern of spirit, something in her willingly pays a difficult price.

> The irresponsive silence of the land,
> The irresponsive sounding of the sea,
> Speak both one message of one sense to me:
> "Aloof, aloof, we stand aloof; so stand
> Thou too aloof, bound with the flawless band
> Of inner solitude; we bind not thee;
> But who from thy self-chain shall set thee free?
> What heart shall touch thy heart? What hand
>   thy hand?"
>
> And I am sometimes proud and sometimes meek
> And sometimes I remember days of old
> When fellowship seemed not so hard to seek
> And all the world and I seemed much less cold,
> And at the rainbow's foot lay surely gold,
> And hope felt strong and life itself not weak.

One recognizes the hallmarks of integrity, and spirit
approves of spirit.

Recognizes how? By signs incompatible with
spiritual hypocrisy—by simplicity, exactness of word

choice, the personal colour which suffuses an idea once that idea has been taken into a mind, later to be given out individualized and fresh. The spirit requires concrete images as bright points of departure. It is a bird rising from its ground-nest.

Christina Rossetti's claim to high poetic distinction is because of her ability to saturate a poem with values beyond temporary considerations, so that one forgets, as one reads, all other values. Genius obeys a hidden law; it has a sweet and self-conditioned reasonableness. Whoever finds her poetry forbidding is like the poet herself when, on a visit to the Continent, she beheld for the first time the high snowy Alps.

"Their sublimity impressed me like want of sympathy," she said, "because my eyes were unaccustomed."

IV

DOROTHY WORDSWORTH

Dorothy Wordsworth is remembered in a deep stillness, "in the thickest part of the wood, undisturbed except by the occasional dropping of snow from the holly boughs." In the imagination of negligent posterity she has taken on the serenity and self-sufficiency of Nature. Her very labour seems pastoral: nailing up honeysuckle, picking berries that grew wild and ripened by streams, baking bread for her brother William. Yet, in this retirement, among scenes not extraordinary, and with eyes made like ours, she saw so much more. To those who know her only casually she appears to have run a narrow course, with a far, fair prospect, and her name stirs in the breast a delicate envy.

But what folly is a little knowledge. Her tragedy was no less real for being mute to the end of her life.

At Alfoxden there were presentiments, there were signs. Perhaps by slow degrees she foresaw her fate. At dusk a flock of sheep went by the house all white and soft and fleecy, but in the morning she saw that moss had been rubbed from the palings, and locks of wool hung there, spotted with red.

To call off the places where she lived is to invoke a train of shadows: Cockermouth, where she was born in 1771 and at seven left motherless; Halifax, where her mother's cousin Elizabeth Threlkeld raised her gloomily, and she heard of her father's death; Penrith, where she endured irritable grandparents and a carping uncle; Forncett, in Uncle William's rectory, where she mourned her absent brothers, Richard, John, Kit, and most of all William, at Cambridge; Halifax again, where she stood by William, stanchly, when the family raged over his half-French daughter Caroline by Annette Beaupuis; Racedown in Dorset, where she and William struggled against poverty, for the income from Raisley Calvert's £900 legacy was insufficient, and the child Basil Montagu hardly paid for his board and keep, and hewing wood hurt the back, and cabbages were a meagre diet; Alfoxden, where they were wonderfully happy discussing the principles of poetry with Coleridge, who walked over from Nether Stowey, but where the neighbors were hostile, whispering "queer," and their landlady refused to renew their year's lease; Germany, where they spent six months with Coleridge and saw an obscure and evil fate gathering like a thundercloud over his impulsive, brilliant head; Sockburn, home of the orphaned Hutchinsons, where she felt an intimation of forlorn grief in the more than friendly attachment of William for Mary, and of Coleridge for Sara. . . .

The morning she and William arrived at Dove Cottage, she ran in ecstasy to see Grasmere Lake and lofty Nab Scar. The quarters were small and neighbors too near, but the gardens had exciting possibilities, and the regions within walking distance were perfect—she would not have them changed by a leaf or a stone. Old Molly Fisher, the servant, beamed at her short, slight mistress in a striped gown and quaint straw bonnet. She was not pretty, but had lovely wild darting eyes and, according to De Quincey, "a glancing quickness in all her movements." And, "her speech," he said, "often suffered in clearness and steadiness from the agitation of her excessive organic sensibility."

Those three years at Grasmere brought so pure a happiness, a superstitious person might have been warned. .

When household tasks were finished they took long walks, Dorothy observing the small perfections of Nature, William meditating "like a rapt god." They understood each other without words, as they understood the lakes and mountains. When he was discouraged, she believed in him and—what was more concrete —laid open her exquisite notebook for his reference in making poems. Love for her brother, she said, was "the building up of my being, the light of my path." If he went away for as much as one night her heart was dead in her side till she heard his returning footsteps on the cobblestones. Once Coleridge, after eleven o'clock, found her in the moonlit garden, watching the undulating vale bathed in silvery and ineffable light. The great poet who lay asleep upstairs was not more sensitive, nor quickly aware. But like Antigone, without complaining, she completely sank her life in the life of her brother. This is a typical notation in her *Journal:* "Saturday, 23rd. William was composing all morning. I shelled peas, gathered beans. . . ."

Between the peas and beans she put down her changing impressions:

"The sea of a sober grey, streaked by the deeper grey clouds. The half dead sound of the near sheep-bell in the hollow of the sloping coombe, exquisitely soothing."

And:

"At once the clouds seemed to cleave asunder, and left the moon in the centre of a black-blue vault. She sailed along, followed by multitudes of stars, small, and bright, and sharp."

And again:

"Grasmere Lake a beautiful image of stillness, clear as glass, reflecting all things. The wind was up, and the waters sounding. The lake of a rich purple, the fields a soft yellow, the copses red-brown. . . . The church and buildings, how quiet they were!"

And in the winter:

"It snowed all day. A very deep snow. The brooms were very beautiful, arched feathers with wiry stalks pointed to the end, smaller and smaller. They waved gently with the weight of the snow."

And,

"Ambleside looked excessively beautiful as we came out— like a village in another country."

And in May:

"We sat in the orchard. The young bull-finches in parti- coloured raiment poise themselves like wire-dancers or tum- blers, shaking the twigs and dashing off the blossoms. There is one primrose in the orchard. The stitchwort is fading. The vetches are in abundance, blossoming and seeding. That pretty little wavy-looking dial-like yellow flower, the speed- well. . . . It has rained sweetly for two hours and a half; the air is very mild. The heckberry blossoms are dropping off fast, almost gone; barberries are in beauty; snowballs coming forward."

And again:

"I found a strawberry blossom in a rock. I uprooted it rashly"—to transplant in her garden—"and felt as if I had been committing an outrage, so I planted it again." She adds, "It will have but a stormy life of it, but let it live if it can."

To her who was predisposed to solitude, William was not a companion so much as an extension of herself. Very happy people see every threadlike vein on a leaf— and very sad people. Dorothy Wordsworth passed so quickly from the one to the other.

Mary Hutchinson had just departed after a long visit when William followed her in haste. Dorothy, now in her early thirties, sat on a flat stone by the sullen lake, weeping as if all hope were gone forever. In a sense it was. She had hoped to be eyes, ears, hands and a heart to her adored William. Mary was good and sweet, an exceptional woman; their friendship had lasted since childhood and been tested many times. But Dorothy wept on her solitary stone.

What force drove men and women together? William and Annette. William and Mary. Coleridge, with a dutiful if bustling wife, and Sara Hutchinson. Two and two. But she was only one. . . .

She remembered the first time she ever saw Coleridge, a pale thin young man swinging along the honeysuckle lane at Racedown, leaping a fence and approaching across a pathless field. She remembered his sudden rapturous appearances at Alfoxden—the bread and cheese shared among them, the brown mug, his marvelous full voice reading "The Ancient Mariner." She remembered so well a serene afternoon, on the way to Stowey, when he and she had lain sidelong on the rich turf, gazing at the beautiful landscape till it melted, and come home in the twilight, their faint shadows going before them. . . .

Ah, Coleridge. . . . The shadows were getting denser and longer. Something had happened to him which baffled her. Not Sara Hutchinson. Sara was nothing. He imagined she was something, with her pensive moods and long pale fine hair; but she was only an incident, an excuse. It was something else which was turning his old glorious tumultuous self to apathy, and weighting his tongue. Could he have talked once, in excitement and wonder, about all three of them immigrating to St. Michael's in the Azores?—talked about sowing a forest with blue laburnum? She saw the slack figure and bloodshot eyes, heard the self-loathing, and one day his cry, "Sinking, sinking, sinking—I feel that I am sinking." It was too terrible that this should happen to Coleridge, of all people. What would she not do for him! But she could do nothing. Once—she remembered exactly where they had been, and the warmth of his voice, and the quick tribute of his eyes—he had said she was exquisite. Exquisite—*she!*

William Wordsworth and Mary Hutchinson were to be married at Gallow Hill in October. The night before she quit Dove Cottage Dorothy wrote in her *Journal:*

"We walked backwards and forwards on the White Moss path. . . . O, beautiful place! Dear Mary, William. The hour is come. I must prepare to go. The swallows, I must leave them, the well, the garden, the roses, all. Dear creatures! they sang last night after I was in bed; seemed to be singing to one another, just before they settled to rest for the night. Well, I must go. Farewell."

She knew that she was saying farewell to much more than the swallows.

The day of the wedding she was too ill to attend, and after the ceremony at the church, when she kissed William, he had to support her, to keep her from falling. Out of pity he took her for a six-weeks tour of Scotland, with Coleridge—the same three whom Coleridge at Alfoxden had called "one soul." But time had not moved backward, and all was changed. . . .

Mary's children followed fast, once they got started: Johnny, Dorothy (or Sissy), Tom, and Catharine (or Kate). The little house was a maelstrom of activity, and from morning till night Dorothy gave herself without restraint. She had no time to read, or even think. Coleridge, mysteriously threatened by some obscure evil, was crossing to the Continent, and exhausted, she sat up late copying the poems, by William, which Coleridge had said he would like to take with him, at her heart a painful sweet pressure. Then her brother John's ship the *Abergavenny* sank to the bottom of the sea, and she remembered, acutely, how good he had been, how kind, and her eyes were red with weeping. And then her old loyal servant Molly took sick and was bewildered, and could not work any more. And then it was necessary to move from Dove Cottage, the walls of which they had all but burst, to Allen Bank, which was larger; but the chimneys smoked dreadfully.

But everything else would have been easy—easy—if Coleridge, home from the Continent, had not tried to avoid them. At last his awful secret was out. The idea of opium made Dorothy shudder. It was worse, even, than she had feared: he who had stood so high had fallen to the very lowest depths. But—he was having trouble with lectures in London? He wanted to found a weekly, *The Friend?* He must come and live with them, by all means; they would help him in any way they could.

During this anxious period, and about the time that a third son was born to Mary and William, little Catharine, the merriest of the children, became paralyzed.

Then Coleridge seemed wilfully to bring on a misunderstanding with William, and one day, on his way to Nether Stowey, passed their house with face grimly averted. That day was Dorothy's doom. How could she live in a world in which such a thing could happen? If it was consolation, she told herself, nothing could ever be added to this extreme of suffering. But soon two things were added. Catharine, whom she loved tenderly, died. And six months later little blue-eyed Tom, the one who would never quarrel, died too.

There were many friends to offer comfort: De Quincey, Lamb, Robinson, Hazlitt, Southey. . . . But on the two short graves the autumn leaves were piling, and in sorrow the family left Grasmere for Rydal Mount.

A letter written in the old eloquent impetuous manner, and striking unmistakably the profound and affectionate note, was received from Coleridge. But it was too late.

Forty-two more years stretched ahead for Dorothy Wordsworth. Before her death in 1855 she would take trips to the Continent, to Scotland, and the Isle of Man;

would swell her notebook with beautiful writing; would have the joy of seeing Mary's remaining children grow up; would bear further faithful witness to William. Fires would be lit, food eaten; she would be refreshed by "drenches of sleep." Nature would not fail her, and she in her loving vigils would not fail Nature.

But the letter from Coleridge, that day in December, 1813, only blew the last spark before the smothering out. A flame which he might have kept alive was dead. Only in the terrible last years of her life when the faculties of her rare mind went into eclipse, and all darkened, was the long inward struggle made visible.

Did she remember the heron she had seen years ago at Rydal, swimming with only its neck out of water, which beat its lovely white wings, and was long in getting loose?

In those last years, very mercifully, she remembered nothing.

V

SAPPHO

"I DO not expect," said Sappho, "to touch the heavens with my two arms," but that is what she did. We see the graceful movement from afar, in time and space, but distinctly, for the sunlight which baths the figure is clear and fine, being Greek. What was her face like? It stares back at us from the green-mouldered coins of Lesbos: intelligent, lean and passionate. Except for the especially high-bridged nose, one might meet it on the streets of the Western World today. But she was writing poetry before Zoroaster, or Confucius, or Gautama Buddha, and six hundred years before Christ.

Strangely enough, time has not been her enemy so much as Christians: Gregory, Bishop of Constantinople, who ordered her nine immortal books burned in 380 A. D., and Pope Gregory VII, who completed the devout work in 1073, with a roaring bonfire in Rome. These reverend ecclesiastics asserted in choler that she made the love of each other more attractive than the love of God.

Fate, the creation and therefore the friend of the Greeks, outwitted the bishop and the pope. Sappho's poems, written, at first, on waxed wooden blocks and, later, on newly discovered papyrus, have survived by quotation in Greek and Roman writings, and by accident in an Egyptian dumping ground, covered over for centuries by dry sand. Patient deciphering has salvaged one complete poem, "Hymn to Aphrodite," quoted by Dionysius of Halicarnassus in 25 B. C.; one nearly complete poem, "Peer of the Gods," quoted in an anonymous treatise, "On the Sublime"; and about a hundred and seventy fragments and mutilations. "The dark backward and abysm of time" has rendered up a part of its treasure; and Sappho is no longer a legend to us, but a woman.

Born in Eresus on Lesbos about 635 B. C., the poet was taken as a child to Mitylene, famous then as now for sweet wine, and then though not now for beautiful women. It is probable, from vague allusions in Herodotus, that her father Scamandronymus was of noble blood, and rich, and that, when Sappho was six years old, he corked up the wine bottles of his trade and died. Suidas does not tell us at what age she married Cercolas, "a man of great wealth who sailed from Andros." But she had a daughter, named Cleïa or Cleis after her mother; and as a young widow began to teach dancing and the popular chanting of epithalamia by choruses of young girls.

One of Sappho's fragments says that to her "all lovely things are pure and holy." Does it matter what form her love of these pupils and companions took? For we cannot know. Ovid's words, often used for condemnation, can be used equally well for acquittal: "What lore did Sappho teach but how to love maidens? Yet Sappho was safe." Certainly the story of her love for Phaon and fatal leap from a cliff is bald-faced myth. She says in one place that Alcaeus, the other renowned poet of Lesbos, was her lover, and when Alcaeus murmurs, "Violet-weaving, pure, softly-smiling Sappho, I would say something but shame restrains me," she rebukes him, saying, "If you had a desire of noble or beautiful things . . . shame would not possess your eyes, but you would speak of it justly."

She died an old woman with "ten thousand wrinkles." When young she had said, once, sadly, "Gentle ladies, you will remember till old age what we did together in our brilliant youth!" And, "To die is an evil. So consider the gods—else they would die." But when she felt the hour approaching, she said to Gongyla, "Long it cannot be," and when Gongyla asked how she knew, replied,

"Hermes came in, and looking upon him I said, 'O Master, we are utterly lost. For I swear by the blessed Aphrodite that I care naught any more that I have been lifted up to prosperity, but a longing to die has seized me. O set me in the dewy field. . . .'"

Quietly she reproved her weeping daughter. "It is not right that in the house of song there should be mourning; such things befit us not."

Her mood and attitude were Greek: everything in its place, a true and balanced proportion, reason gauging, correcting and saving the emotions. But Sappho was not the over-refined creature later imitators have suggested. One of her wedding songs lapses into crude raillery. And she is capable of bitterness: "Those whom I treat well harm me most." When her brother Charaxus ransomed the beautiful Egyptian courtesan Rhodopis, notorious in the ancient world, she wrote in anger, "You swarthy she-dog, setting your ill-smelling snout to the ground, pursue other prey!" We see her, across the ages, washing at a cold spring and anointing her skin with costly myrrh, and drinking a liquor made from roasted nuts, and wearing a quince-coloured robe dyed with the juice of boxwood, and being a little vain about it, and very human.

Like the oleander and wild pomegranate of Lesbos, she was vivid; like the marble cliffs, inviolable; like the tideless Aegean, deep. In life as in art the appropriate thing is the beautiful, and the beautiful the satisfy-ing. "For nourishing a contented spirit," she said, "I clearly know that in me the blessed gods are present."

Curious that the greatest woman poet was the first in point of time. Indeed, except for Alcaeus, she was the first lyric poet of either sex. Of the great, only Homer and Hesiod and the Hebraic David preceded her. The inferior Erinna was not her pupil, as is commonly sup-posed, but flourished perhaps two hundred years later, wrote less (she died at nineteen), and unlike Sappho in hexameters. The Ancients held the memory of Sappho in respect, as something matchless and rare. She was known as "The Poetess," and Homer as "The Poet."

In the *Phaedrus* Plato calls her "Sappho the beautiful"; and in an epigram, "the tenth Muse." Solon, hearing one of her poems recited, prayed not to die till he had learned it by heart. Pinytus declared that "the bones and mute name of Sappho the grave holds, but her wise words are imperishable." The wonder is, if the fragments are so fine, what were the whole poems? Could any contemporary poet, if splintered to pieces, prove greatness? Sappho's influence is like the light of a star: from an enormous distance it reaches us unerringly, its quality not changed. Twenty-five hundred years of civilization separate her from us, but we have not learned to be more sensitive to infinitesimal differences, or more fastidious. "I have loved delicacy. . . ."

Such a woman could not have escaped love, on an island of grey-green olive groves, and fountains, and banked cyclamen, samphire and wild rosemary, and tuneful nightingales, and warm air from a restless sea. For her, the meaning of Nature was inseparable from her own meaning. "But the hearts of the doves became cold, and they dropped beside them their wings." This is more than observation; it is identification. And,

"Hesperus, you bring all that the bright dawn scattered: you bring the sheep, you bring the goat, you bring to the mother her child."

The strong are tender, thus, and the great, simple. "All-hearing night," she says, coining the perfect epithet.

And, "Sleep streams down." And, "Spring's messenger, the sweet-voiced nightingale." And, "Night's black sleep was shed upon their eyes." And, "Now Eros has shaken my thoughts, like a wind among highland oaks."

Eros and the oaks; love and nature, suggesting each other. In all literature there are no descriptions of love more powerful than in Sappho's poems.

"When I see you but for a moment my tongue is broken, and a languid fire runs under my flesh, and with my eyes I see nothing, and my ears ring. A sweat pours over me, and trembling seizes every limb; I am paler than grass, and appear to be almost dead . . ."

The physiology and psychology of love cannot be imagined; only recorded. "Love, fatal creature. . ." "Now love the limb-loosener sweeps me away. . ." "Love much whiter than an egg. . ." Love "weaver of fictions." "Love the wild beast." She has felt the bliss, the pangs, the revenges. "I know not what to do; my thoughts are double." And then, "I long and I seek. . ." And,

"The moon is set and the Pleiades gone; it is midnight, and time is going fast, but I lie alone."

Then the mood shifts, for a hope has been fulfilled:

"You have come: you have done well. I longed for you: and you have inflamed my heart already burning with desire. Hail to us, many times hail, and for as long as we were parted."

Then, more triumphantly,

"Some say an army of horsemen is the fairest sight on this sluggish black earth, others an army of foot-soldiers, and others a navy of ships, but I say it is the one you love."

Translated fragments are true to the fundamentals of her thought, but the flowing Greek metre, the enravishing, right words, the pause, the emphasis, are lost.

Fortunately there is excess in greatness: it can lose more than mediocrity possesses, and still be great.

Sappho has influenced a long line of poets: among the Greeks, Meleager and Theocritus, among the Romans, Catullus and Lucretius, and, stepping across to the English, Sir Philip Sidney in his *Arcadia,* Ben Jonson who stole a line about nightingales, and, in recent times, Swinburne, and, among contemporary Americans, Edwin Arlington Robinson. Imitating the strophe which Sappho perfected, they tend to forget that she used many metres, among others, the alcaic, dactylic, choriambic, glyconic, and ionic. But she is unique: her charm and power are derived from more than a technical facility—from a childlike mind: in other words, consummate art with no art at all.

And of course, since every intelligent person knows what he is, how deficient, and how endowed, she knew her worth. To have protested otherwise would have been falsely modest. Sappho says,

"I have received true prosperity from the golden Muses, and when I die shall not be forgot."

How different her indictment of a woman of low aims:

"You shall lie dead, nor shall there be any memory to anyone of you, after; for you have no share of the roses of Pieria, but shall wander unseen even in Hades' house, flitting amid dim corpses."

Sappho's tortoise-shell lyre of four strings, with a cross-piece joining two great goat's horns, is dust, and the hand which plucked it.

But the music persists.

VI

GEORGE SAND

GEORGE SAND

GEORGE SAND, in her youth, ministered to the sick of the town of La Châtre and, because she was dressed in boy's clothes, was repaid by calumny.

"Overcome by despair," she wrote of the incident years later, "I would urge my horse into the blackness of the night. With the goad of the spur in his flank, he bounded ahead and began to run, ears and nostrils tense. We shot like an arrow through one of those great squalls which sweep the plain and, taking a man by surprise, whirl him around, forcing him to retreat. Clinging to the neck of my horse I breasted those winds, and he, feeling them cleave his chest, quivered as if struck by a whip, and whirlwinds of dry leaves crackled around and beat up into my face. I howled like a mad-woman in the midst of the storm, 'Here I am! Here I am! It is my turn to be judged!'"

And in old age, when everything had happened to her which was going to happen, she wrote,

"By some freak of destiny I am stronger and more active than I was in youth. I can walk farther. I can stay awake longer. My body has remained as supple as a glove. I go bathing in icy water and find it pleasant. I am absolutely calm. I no longer live in myself. My heart has gone into my children and my friends. And, since I can bear the evil in my life and appreciate the good, I am not in the least interesting. ... It is a mistake to regard age as a downhill grade toward dissolution. The reverse is true. As one grows older one climbs with surprising strides. Meanwhile, and nevertheless, one approaches the journey's end. But the end is a goal, not a catastrophe."

Between these two states of mind lay her mature life. One may question her greatness as a writer, but not as a human being. She had enemies; she had lovers, and friends. Count d'Dorsay called her "a very dear woman, and the first man of our times." Her contemporary Charlotte Brontë was not without discernment in comparing her to Balzac:

"Truly—I like George Sand better. Fantastic, fanatical, unpractical enthusiast as she often is—far from truthful as are many of her views of Life—misled as she is apt to be by her feelings—George Sand has a better nature . . . her brain is larger—her heart warmer. . . . Most of her very faults spring from the excess of her good qualities; it is this excess which has often hurried her into difficulty, which has prepared for her enduring regret. But I believe her mind is of that order which disastrous experience teaches without weakening. . . . The longer she lives the better she will grow. . . ."

The terrific energy which governed her life multiplied her prose works to a hundred and ten: novels, journals, plays, pamphlets. They are loose in construction and sometimes coarse in grain, but they win by honesty, humility, fearlessness, and sheer emotional drive.

Aurore Dupin, born in 1804, was the daughter of a low-class mother, Sophie Delaborde, and an aristocratic father, Maurice Dupin, who married just in time to spare her illegitimacy. Then the father was killed in a fall from his horse, and the august grandmother, who had been Aurore de Saxe, bribed Sophie the milliner, daughter of a birdseller, to go back to Paris, and took to her capacious and correct bosom the nondescript child. But the child cried for Mamma, and, as punishment, was packed off to a staid convent. Many years later this child, grown up, watched the death of this grandmother, Countess Dupin, descendant of a king of Poland, first cousin to the former Dauphine of France, natural aunt of three kings of France, and daughter of the great military genius, Maurice de Saxe. She lay on a magnificent bed of silk and priceless lace, which smelled of rose, and left all her property to her namesake.

Count Villeneuve, a cousin, offered to adopt the heiress into his distinguished family. But she preferred her derelict mother. This meant being embroiled in Sophie's vulgarity; meant homesickness for "Nohant," the estate she had been willed; meant (eventually) marrying Casimir Dudevant.

Heine has called that solid Gascon soldier a Chinese pagoda, and his ignorant eyes, porcelain. By her marriage to him Aurore lost everything, including her independence. Casimir promptly chopped down her favorite trees at "Nohant," changing all that she loved. When she grew melancholy he was irritable; when she laughed gaily, struck her in the face. But she paid the debts he contracted, and she renounced, in all but a highly idealistic way, a sensitive young lawyer, Aurelian de Seze, whom she had met and loved, dutifully passing on his letters to her husband.

Then one day she heard him soliciting a servant girl—the third, and there had been a child. And she noticed on his desk a letter addressed to herself, to be opened in case of death. Behind the silence, the cruelty, was there love? She split the seal, in her anxiety to find out; but what she read was pure vitriol. Secure in the knowledge that her son Maurice and daughter Solange had a trustworthy tutor, Aurore Dupin Dudevant took the diligence to Paris.

Thus, after nine years, she regained liberty—though not her chateau at "Nohant," her house in Paris, nor half a million francs. She did not complain. She was intoxicated by the concerts, the National Library, the Louvre; and elated when Henri de Latouche, editor of *Figaro,* promised seven francs a column for all of her writings which he could use. Nor, when she earned only fifteen francs in a month, was she discouraged. The voluminous skirts of the period were expensive and soon bedraggled, so she adopted the trousers and blouse of a student. Since the Baroness Dudevant could not buy cheap gallery tickets, she preferred to be a student, anyway.

Jules Sandeau, twenty years old, from her own province of Berry, collaborated with her on a novel called *Rose and Blanche,* signed Jules Sand. After she had returned from a visit to "Nohant," where she was treated like an undesirable alien, they became lovers. Why not? she said. Was she not the same as divorced? She was through with appearances, and free.

Free to love and to work. Her novel *Indiana,* signed George Sand, surprised the publisher no less than the author by being an enormous success. Then *Valentine,* then *Lélia,* then a long line of novels which were read, warred over, and branded as shocking, for the ideas which they embodied were a hundred years ahead of her time.

But fame was not peace. George Sand worried about her son Maurice, in a Paris military school, and about her daughter Solange, who was with her now, petulant and wilful. And one day, returning unexpectedly to her apartment, she found Jules in the arms of a laundress. She did not storm; but paid his rent to the end of the year, and, since they had planned a trip to Italy, gave him the money to go alone.

Her friend, the actress Marie Dorval, argued that the only cure for love was more love—and she met Prosper Mérimée. The affair lasted a week, no longer, and then for months she regretted her mistake. Still, she knew it was love she wanted more than anything else in the world.

One night at a dinner given by François Buloz, editor of the *Revue des Deux Mondes,* she sat next to the famous young poet whom two months before she had refused to meet, Alfred de Musset. As he ate he glanced covertly at the slim woman whose "eyes devoured her face." She wore an Oriental gown, that was out of fashion, with a short jacket of braided gold, and a strange turban. "How small she is!" he thought. Her hands were the smallest, whitest, and most troubling he had ever seen. She noticed the extreme cut of his green coat, and his curled hair. A handsome aristocrat, she reflected—but the kind that thought one thing and professed another. No, she did not like dandies.

But two weeks later, "It was his tears," she wrote Sainte-Beuve, "which made me yield."

After an interval in her Paris apartment, the two went for a holiday at Fontainebleau, where she delighted him by wearing a blue student's blouse, riding horseback, dancing, singing Berry peasant songs, imitating birds, and teaching him the names of the flowers of the fields and woods. The only drawback was, he would not let her work, and she became restless. "In Italy," he promised. But when at last they stepped from a gondola at the Hotel Danielli in Venice, after a month of rattling stagecoaches and pitching boats, he cried in sudden temper, "George, you are the most tiresome woman I know!" She was so ill she had to go to bed; but they owed money for the trip, and she began to write. He retaliated for this inconsideration with low women and strong drink, and one evening at dinner spoke coldly: "I beg your pardon, George; I have made a mistake.

I do not love you." "We no longer love each other," she said, as haughtily.

If only it had been true.

Then Alfred decided that he was going insane, but the Italian Dr. Pagello, when called in, diagnosed the symptoms as typhoid fever complicated by delirium tremens. The shrieking patient went into convulsions and tried to strangle George, who nursed him night and day. She had sixty lire, and drugs were needed. If she slept at all, it was on the sofa in her clothes. When Alfred found out that she was having an affair with Dr. Pagello, back and forth he swung, in wild moods of devil and saint. Then, dramatizing self-sacrifice, he surrendered her to Pagello. But now she definitely wanted Alfred. Back in Paris, in vain she begged the two jealous men for a three-cornered friendship. When she finally let Pagello go and took Alfred again, he reviled her for unfaithfulness. They separated, and made up, and separated. "Ah George, what a love! I don't know whether I live or eat or walk or breathe or speak." And she,

"I have died day by day, now I die minute by minute. Cruel child, why did you love me after having hated me? What mystery fulfils itself in you each week? . . . Never again, blue eyes, will you gaze at me. . . . Oh God, God, if you would give me back a single day of the happiness you have taken from me!"

But she knew that for love she had lost hard-won

liberty, and at last, worn out, she renounced the only man who had ever given her complete joy.

Nature, as always, healed her. But should she take the advice of friends and go back to her husband?— live with a man she did not love? No, she would keep her sex relations pure. So she appealed to Michel of Bourges, the great Berry lawyer, who had an ugly face under a knotted handkerchief. There was no such thing as a divorce, he said. There should be, she said. But there was not, so what did she want? A judicial separation, she said. Very well; but would her husband contest the suit? Not if she settled money on him and gave him her Paris house. Michel hardly heard. He was thinking that he must convert this woman to the cause of the Republic, and began an impassioned speech. But she had always believed in a Republic, she said enthusiastically.

At the trial Casimir, breaking his word, accused her of every vice. It was a terrible ordeal for George largely because the fate of her children hung in balance. "I am good, no matter what they say," was her position, "and what they say does not bother me." Thanks to the eloquence of Michel, the case was decided in her favour. Casimir then appealed from La Châtre to the Royal Court at Bourges and, at sensational exposures, the jury hung; but after all, the case was settled out of court, Maurice going to the husband, Solange to the wife. Later, when Casimir's mother died, George claimed that her husband, having come into his own inheritance, no longer needed half of hers. The court did not concur. But for forty thousand francs Casimir surrendered his right to the Paris house and Maurice.

She was thirty-four, and would live to be seventy-two, but so much was gone forever. She busied herself with the children she loved to distraction; and, entangled with Michel, began to write, between novels, pamphlets for his Republic. When asked to contribute to *Le Monde,* a penniless radical newspaper, she wrote the "Letters à Marcie," proclaiming the equality of women with men. After the domineering Michel, there was Maurice's tutor, Félicien Mallefille, and then Frederic Chopin the composer.

Chopin, who had just lost a Polish woman he loved, was sad, ill and destitute. What joy to George Sand to be needed! But during their winter in a abandoned Majorcan monastery, it rained continually on the orange trees, the lemon and the fig, and Chopin's special piano was detained by the customs, and the country people of Valldemosa gossipped unmercifully. Still, George wrote, and Chopin played on a borrowed piano. One year of intimacy was followed by seven of chastity. He came to think of "Nohant" as his home, and of Maurice and Solange as his children.

The trouble started over Solange—there was bound to be trouble over Solange. She was, like her father, arrogant, cruel, very lazy, and determined to achieve prominence at any cost. Her mother's talent she hated, because she could not compete with it. When about to sign a marriage contract with the eminent Preaulx family, she switched her affections to Clésinger, a sculptor. George forestalled an elopement, but when Clésinger hinted at an indiscretion, implored them to hasten the marriage. There was no peace after that. Jealous of her cousin Augustine who lived at "Nohant," Solange charged her with being Maurice's mistress. Jealous of Maurice, Clésinger attacked him with a hammer, and George, intervening, was struck on the breast and, staggering back, saw Solange smiling. Chopin, also jealous of Maurice, took the side of Solange and Clésinger, and so, in time, when the poison of suspicion had worked, was completely estranged from George. But on his deathbed he murmured in sorrow, "She told me I should not die except in her arms."

Such a life might have destroyed a lesser woman. George Sand escaped to larger considerations. The Second Republic had been established in 1848, and again she wrote pamphlets, giving the proceeds to the unemployed. A cartoon of the times shows an attractive woman, as tall as Gulliver among the Lilliputians, cracking a big whip over a lot of dancing politicians, who scurry for shelter under her skirts. In 1851, at Napoleon's *coup d'état,* George expected imprisonment or exile. But instead of hiding she went to beg Prince Napoleon to exonerate her friends, and he did, and she turned to play-writing. It was always so. When one life died, another was born.

A play about the peasants of Berry, *François Le Champi,* was followed by other successes. She was not a great playwright; knew very little about dramatic construction; but always she gave an impression of throbbing life.

At "Nohant," in their private theatre, she had the amusement without the burdens of art. Maurice carved marionettes for a Punch and Judy show, and George made tiny clothes from scraps of cotton and silk.

One day Maurice brought home to Nohant a friend, Alexandre Manceau, a pupil of Delacroix and a fine engraver. "He helps everyone, thinks of everyone," she noted, "but himself." Before long he was classifying her manuscripts, doing the bookkeeping, answering her letters, enlarging the theatre, building Maurice a studio, putting on her desk every night a glass of sweetened water for the long literary vigil, and, when she went to Paris, buying the tickets and packing the trunks. She expressed a wish to get away from all but her own thoughts, and he purchased for her, and repaired and furnished, a cottage in the pastoral village of Gargilesse.

After a few years Solange and her husband obtained a legal separation; their lovely little daughter Jeanne died of an apparently minor ailment; and at thirty-nine Maurice married dowerless Lina Calamatta.

Then Manceau developed symptoms of consumption,

and Maurice quarrelled with him, and George had to choose between her son and her closest friend. Have I a choice? she asked. Manceau had served her fifteen years, and was ill. They procured a pretty little house at Palaiseau near Paris, and for a mournful year she took care of him. After his death she wrote Flaubert, "To love in spite of everything, I think that is the answer to the enigma of the universe."

When in old age she returned to "Nohant," Marco her grandson had died. Gabrielle still was very small, but her sister Aurore—the fourth Aurore—prattled endlessly.

"Which do you like better, the Trojans or the Greeks?" asked Grandmother.

"The Greeks. Pallas Athene was with the Greeks, so they must have had justice on their side," said Aurore. "Grandmother, why do you like the Trojans?"

"Because they are to be pitied."

Aurore understood quite well.

This Aurore, George's last passion! Friends like Sainte-Beuve, Liszt, Heine, the younger Dumas, Gautier, Renan, Taine, Bernhardt, the Goncourts, Prince Jerome, Fleury, and Flaubert, shrivelled to insignificance. "Aurore is a treasure, a little wonder. . . ."

At sixty-six, when the Franco-German War broke, the indomitable women wrote in her *Journal,* "It will pass like a squall over a lake." She lived through the War, and the Commune, and into the Third Republic.

One day in 1876 a doctor who had come to treat Maurice was summoned upstairs, and found George Sand, who was seventy-two, sitting at her writing-table with a pen in her hand and a cigarette in her mouth—smiling.

A few days later, from her bed, she asked for her grandchildren.

"Look at me, my darlings," she entreated.

The small faces were upturned.

And she cried with her last conscious breath,

"I love you, I adore you."

VII

JANE AUSTEN

JANE AUSTEN

In her lifetime (1775-1817) she was plain Jane Austen, not to be criticized, for she kept the proprieties, nor particularly lauded—for what was remarkable about her? But since her quietly tragic death by tuberculosis at the age of forty-two, voice after voice has been lifted in astonishment, in admiration, in strong, unhysterical praise. Archbishop Whately began it; Coleridge, Tennyson, and Macaulay carried it forward. Scott said, "That young lady had a talent for describing the involvements, feelings and characters of ordinary life which is to me the most wonderful I ever met with." Disraeli read *Pride and Prejudice* seventeen times. Thus the covertly satiric and genial clergyman's daughter who required only twenty-one years of life before the immortal Mr. Bennett and Elizabeth Bennett and Mr. Darcy matured in her brain, required over a hundred years to be universally accounted a classic—which is like an irony of her own devising.

Jane Austen's life was as unelaborate as her prose style. She was born on a cold day in December at the parsonage of Steventon, in Hampshire, England, and there were six other children to gape at the new baby in the crib and solicit her attention with odd clucking noises. The father was George Austen, a rector who preferred Pope to preaching the gospel. The mother Cassandra Leigh was the niece of Theophilus Leigh, a dry humorist who was for fifty years master of Balliol. At an early age Jane began to toy with her pen, with no other motive, apparently, than to amuse her family. When she was twenty-six the household moved to Bath, the fashionable watering-place of the time, which no normal young lady could enter without extreme excitement. Whether the flutterings were inward or outward depended on the temperament of the young lady. Jane's were strictly invisible.

A shadow fell too soon on this brightness, but what shadow does not? After four years in Bath her father died, and Jane and her mother and sister Cassandra, in the house in Green Park Buildings, listened to their unsupplemented footsteps. In a kind of orderly panic they moved to Southampton, to share a house with Captain Francis Austen, and a few years later retreated, still further, to Chawton, Hampshire.

But it is in Winchester Cathedral that a black slab in the floor arrests the feet of pilgrims, and sunlight enflames a memorial window. In Winchester Jane Austen sought medical aid in 1817, and there two months later, in the gentlest manner, died, and was buried, long ago—so many springs, so many autumns, so many winters shed on tall Jane Austen, on the lithe figure that loved to dance, the bright hazel eyes, the delicate features, the red-apple colour, the beautiful brown curly hair, under a white cap, frilled. . . .

We examine her novels—*Pride and Prejudice,*

Northanger Abbey, Sense and Sensibility, the fragment called *The Watsons, Mansfield Park, Emma,* and *Persuasion,* all, at first, published anonymously. In these comedies of domestic life in the provinces, people talk, hope, plot, are disappointed, and when everything seems against them, are rescued, are comforted. "The little bit (two inches wide) of ivory on which I work with so fine a brush," she said, "produces little effect after much labour." Little effect in the sense of no passion, no crime, no violence of any kind, including religious ideas. But much incisive effect of character. The people are transparent: they cannot hide their motives and "they are betrayed by what is false within."

Jane Austen's classic restriction of theme has led to a controversy in taste, well illustrated by the divergent views of Charlotte Brontë and Katherine Mansfield, her peers. Says Charlotte Brontë,

"She does her business of delineating the surface of the lives of genteel English people curiously well; there is a Chinese fidelity, a miniature delicacy in the painting: she ruffles the reader by nothing vehement, disturbs him by nothing profound. . . . She no more with her mind's eye beholds the heart of her race than each man with bodily vision sees the heart in his heaving breast. Jane Austen was a complete and most sensible lady, but a very incomplete and rather insensible (not senseless) woman. If this is heresy—I cannot help it."

Pride and Prejudice is, according to her,

"an accurate daguerreotyped portrait of a commonplace face; a carefully fenced, highly cultivated garden, with neat borders and delicate flowers; but no glance of a bright, vivid physiognomy, no open country, no fresh air, no blue hill, no bonny beck. I should hardly like to live with her ladies and gentlemen in their elegant but confined houses."

Katherine Mansfield, on the other hand, wrote Lady Ottoline Morrell:

"M. and I are reading Jane Austen in the evenings—with delight. *Emma* is really a perfect book—don't you feel? I enjoy every page. I can't have enough of Miss Bates or Mr. Woodhouse's gruel or that charming Mr. Knightley. It's such an exquisite comfort to escape from the modern novels I have been forcibly reading. Wretched affairs! This fascinated pursuit of sex adventure is beyond words boring! I am so bored by sex *qua* sex, by the gay dog sniffing round the prostitute's bedroom or by the ultra modern snigger—worse still—that I could die—at least."

Jane Austen did not ask for special privileges because she happened to have the gift of writing. An apology would have come more readily to her lips. If one surprises her in the gabled Steventon parsonage, or the pretty drawing-room at 4 Sidney Place, Bath, or spacious Godmersham Hall, or quaint Chawton Cottage, one never catches her writing. No matter how suddenly one arrives, she has heard the door close or a footstep cross the threshold, and hidden the white sheets covered with black, firm, delicate script, like wrens' feet. Perhaps she is telling a niece or nephew a fairy story.

Perhaps she is throwing spilikins in a perfect circle and picking them off with a steady hand—being famous for getting the ivory ball in the cup a hundred times in succession. More probably she is gathering a ruffle with finest stitches, or working a rose or a bunch of grapes on an embroidery frame. Her hands created as exquisitely as her brain: witness a muslin scarf embellished in satin-stitch, which time has not destroyed. Or she is dusting, boiling jelly, polishing brass, hanging curtains, or keeping the happy family tradition of reading out loud. We have her letters to her beloved sister Cassandra, 1796 to 1816, but alas, Cassandra has expurgated all passages which she considered too intimate for strangers' eyes. But the choicest events in a life are written in the heart, anyway; the clues are faint, if they exist at all, and must be searched out, and guessed at.

Her brothers Francis William and Charles write that the Navy has promoted them—and across a century runs an echoing vibration, the flurry in the family bosom. Jane reads the poet Crabbe and says jocosely, "If I ever married at all I could fancy being Mrs. Crabbe." The letters, unlike the novels, show a decent feminine weakness for clothes. "I believe I shall make my new gown like my robe, but the back of the latter is all in a piece with the tail, and will seven yards enable me to copy it in that respect?" And, "All my money is spent in buying white gloves and pink persian." And,

"I bought some Japan ink and next week begin my operations on my hat, on which you know my principal hopes of happiness depend."

But we know next to nothing about her real hopes for happiness because she did not choose to divulge them. Mary Russell Mitford said that her mother lived in the neighborhood of the Austens and knew Jane as "the prettiest, silliest, most affected, husband-hunting butterfly she ever remembers"—but when Mrs. Mitford married and left home Jane was barely ten years old, and two years later was roundly accused by a cousin of being prim. She herself protests to Cassandra, but too much and too laughingly, that she is a flirt. One tries in vain to conjure something romantic out of Sam Blackall, whom she called "a piece of perfection—noisy perfection." When he married she wrote rather maliciously to her brother Frank:

"I could wish Miss Lewis to be of a silent turn and rather ignorant, but naturally intelligent and wishing to learn, fond of cold veal pies, green tea in the afternoon, and a green window-blind at night."

Posthumous match-making (that affront) is forced to confine itself to Tom Lefroy, later Chief Justice of Ireland, about whom Jane wrote Cassandra, after a ball at Manydown,

"I am almost afraid to tell you how my Irish friend and I behaved. Imagine to yourself everything most profligate and shocking about dancing and sitting down together."

A few days later this badinage started up again.

"At length the day is come on which I am to flirt my last with Tom Lefroy, and when you receive this it will be over. My tears flow as I write at the melancholy idea."

We do not know what happened. He went away, they never again met on intimate terms, and he became engaged to another lady and married her. As an old man nearly ninety he told a young kinsman that, "he had been in love with Jane Austen, but it was a boy's love." Is catastrophe hidden in these facts, about which she joked so lightly and mercilessly? We cannot know. The reason why she laid down her pen for twelve of her best years must remain a mystery. So much decays and falls apart. We might grow tragic over the effacements and permutations of time, but stop ourselves. Jane Austen would not approve. She never admitted that anything was tragic, but turned it into an ironical intuition, a witticism not dark enough nor quite cruel enough to be sardonic, but merry and sober for provoking the intellect's laughter.

She has denied that her characters are real persons: snobbish Mrs. Elton, the overweening and fatuous Lady Catherine de Bourgh, selfish busy Mr. Collins, Lady Middleton whose "reserve was a mere calmness of *manner* with which *sense* had nothing to do," Mr. Allen the country gentleman who "did not care about the garden, and never went into it," Catherine Morland who told Henry Tilney she "could not speak well enough to be unintelligible," Mr. John Dashwood who talked himself out of giving his sisters a thousand pounds apiece, Anne Elliot who "spread purification and perfume" as she walked through Bath, Emma Woodhouse crying "Good God!" and renowned unforgettable Mr. Darcy who

"soon drew the attention of the room by his fine, tall person, handsome features, noble mien, and the report, which was in general circulation within five minutes after his entrance, of his having ten thousand a year . . . till his manners gave a disgust which turned the tide of his popularity; for he was discovered to be proud, to be above his company, and above being pleased."

Lucidly, sharply, without serious wish for revenge, Jane Austen practiced the rare honesty of talking about only what she knew from habit of observation. Her "art of keeping lovers apart in five volumes" (more or less) has been called a "genius of mockery." Nothing escapes her barb, except the British Navy, and it is in danger, for Sir Walter Elliot is made to say that "all officers should be killed off at forty because of their weather-beaten complexions." She loved nothing better than a ball, unless it was to lampoon a ball: "There were very few beauties and such as there were were not very handsome." Still, Elizabeth Bennett, the heroine most like herself, says, "I hope I never ridicule what is wise or good," and we suspect them both, for all their scornful sallies, of the most loving hearts.

When in 1803 Crosbie and Co., London, paid ten pounds for *Northanger Abbey* and then locked it in a safe for as many years, the author may have frowned, but more probably she smiled, for she had a private, unconventional opinion of what was dire and lamentable and what was not.

Her imagination took a thought, polished it off, related it to other thoughts, reduced it to essence—as she lifted the tea caddy, inquired how many sugars, and poured in slow ceremony the pure, bitter, amber stream.

VIII

EMILY BRONTË

Behind the bleak village of Haworth, Yorkshire, behind the sad stone church, mouldering graveyard and lonely parsonage, stretch the moors—pathless and gorse-covered hills, cupping into hollows that shelter thyme and purple heather, and washed by flood-streams of sky. A century ago they were Emily Brontë's.

She had only to pass through an iron turnstile, cross a barren meadow topped by quarries, another turnstile, and she was alone, she was free. Anyone who had followed her would have seen a tall pale dark girl, thin in the blast, with head back and nostrils tense, stopping to look at some fern, or a patch of furze, and then on and on, as though she could never get enough, like something long pent and now liberated. But no one followed. In all that waste no eyes looked out but the lapwing's or the moorcock's. It was so still that when the wind was right she could hear water going over the small stones of the beck. The look of the land changed with the diminishing day. She knew every shift of light. As she walked, she felt a vast, grim, unrelenting and incommunicable joy, and that too became a part of her, and when she died was still in her, unescaped and uncorrupted.

She never willingly left the moors, alienating herself from herself. By being born in Thornton (1818), and not being brought to Haworth till two years later, it was as if that first absence were deeply repented of, and made up for, as far as possible.

Her father, Patrick Brontë, born a Prunty in the county of Down in Ireland, cared nothing for moors; but sat all day in his study, moodily eating his meals there, reading voraciously, and writing verses. First as a weaver, then a schoolmaster, then a tutor, then for four years a student at St. John's College, Cambridge, and now as a poor parson, the Celt had been weaned from the land.

The mother, born Maria Branwell, stayed in bed most of the time, her native Cornwall dreaming in her eyes. Just before she died of cancer she pulled herself up, with difficulty, to watch a servant clean the fireplace "like Cornwall people."

Six in a row, tightly holding hands, the motherless children wandered over the heath, in capes and bonnets: Maria, Elizabeth, Charlotte, Emily, the boy Branwell with red hair curling beneath a peaked cap, and the baby Anne. At home they played games in a tiny box of a "children's study," were instructed by Aunt Elizabeth, who had come from Cornwall to take Mother's place, or trailed Tabby around the kitchen, begging cookies, till they could go out again. But only Emily loved the moors with that undeviating fierceness usually associated with hate.

At six she was sent with her three older sisters to the wretched Clergy Daughters' School at Cowan Bridge, to be dressed in brown holland pinafores and fed on lumpy gruel; and when Maria and Elizabeth sickened there, and died of consumption soon after, she pleaded, even more piteously, to come home. At seventeen, at Miss Wooler's boarding school at Roe Head, where Charlotte was now assistant mistress, she pined and wasted so, for furze and whinstone, for the birch and mountain-ash halfway up the falls, for the loosed and whining east wind, that there was nothing to do but call her back. At twenty-three, she went with Charlotte through London to Brussels, and was out of sight and sound of the moors for nine months, but Charlotte says that she conquered her homesickness at great cost and "almost died of the victory."

Like her prototype Shirley, in Charlotte's book of that name, she had "odd points and grand points." She was unorthodox in her wildness; harsh and incalculable powers worked in her. Monsieur Héger of the Héger Pensionnat, who taught her French and German, said that she "should have been a man—a great navigator. Her powerful reason would have deduced new spheres of discovery from the knowledge of the old; and her strong imperious will would never have been daunted by opposition or difficulty; never have given way but with life." She could impose, on anyone who would listen, any scene, any set of characters, which she wished to create; and, among the eighty or ninety pupils, shone like a light in darkness. Charlotte was intelligent, he thought, but Emily had genius. She disconcerted him, this unsmiling girl who came back at him so obstinately; who wrote brilliant compositions like the one on Harold at the Battle of Hastings, in French, which she had just begun to study; who walked arm in arm with her sister in an outmoded formless skirt and leg-of-mutton sleeves, and for hours said not one word, only looked, and one knew that the sullen crater smothered an awful fire. At the end of the short term both sisters were asked to stay on as teachers; and they used vacation for browsing in the museum, and exploring a quaint countryside.

Then they received an urgent message, and when they arrived home Aunt Elizabeth had gone to the overcrowded graveyard, in her discreet silk dress. But the large bonnet trimmed with ruching which she always wore when she went out, she had not worn it. And her gold snuff-box lay on the table. . . . Their father was almost seventy, and slowly going blind. Crude faithful Tabby was eighty. Since one of them must remain, Emily did. It was not a punishment.

She felt like the dead snuffing sweet air again. Ah, nothing was changed on the moors. Wild ducks rose from the green tussocks of hair grass and golden bent, as she approached; the north wind slashed at her face; wherever she looked stretched sky and her mind went still further—there was no end.

When Charlotte returned from Brussels they talked of founding a private school so that they could support themselves at home. Emily had had a comparatively brief experience of teaching, at Miss Patchett's School for Young Ladies at Law Hill, and loathed it. But they printed a prospectus, and waited. Not one pupil applied.

Then Anne who was tutoring in the same wealthy family as Branwell began to write vague suspicions. It was not the first time Branwell had terrified his doting kin. A child of extraordinary talent, he had grown into a young man without hope, or honour. At the Black Bull Inn of Haworth he drank and gambled, slunk home when Emily warned him that Father was coming, by tapping on the window, and took opium. He had been their god, now he was their reproach. At vacation time he had been nervous, and had spoken mysteriously of treason. Then two things, it is said, reached the parsonage together one day in July: Branwell, looking wild and sick, and a letter from his employer, Mr. Robinson, ordering him to keep away from his wife. Henceforth Branwell's moral and physical decay was rapid. But he died in a milder mood—died standing, with his boots on, they say in Haworth. . . .

One day Charlotte had found and surreptitiously read the copy-book in which Emily wrote her poems, and been excited by the bare purity of this beauty. But Emily was offended that the sacred privacy, tacitly agreed upon since childhood, had been enfringed upon. It took hours to placate her, and weeks to kindle in her a spark of what Charlotte called "honourable ambition." *Poems by Currer, Ellis and Acton Bell* was printed at the author's expense. Charlotte's poems are undistin-

guished, meek Anne's scarcely better, but Emily's are
the powerful cry of a nature which cannot be plumbed
so deep it is and true.

> No coward soul is mine,
> No trembler in the world's storm-troubled sphere:
> I see Heaven's glories shine,
> And faith shines equal, arming me from fear.
>
> * * * *
>
> There is not room for Death,
> Nor atom that his might could render void,
> Thou—Thou art Being and Breath,
> And what Thou art may never be destroyed.

This gaunt young woman beating a rug in the garden
by a lonely currant bush, or kneeling on the floor to
count apples, or abruptly leaving the room to avoid a
stranger, this taciturn young woman who wrote in easy
rhythms about wind, sun, flowers, birds, and the open
space of the moors and the closed space of the grave,
belonged to that thinned rank of human beings who are
overcome by nothing and saddened by very little: they
have mastered the world by mastering themselves.

> And am I wrong to worship where
> Faith cannot doubt, nor hope despair,
> Since my own soul can grant my prayer?

And,

> So hopeless is the world without,
> The world within I doubly prize.

And after death, when "dawns the Invisible,"

O dreadful is the check—intense the agony—
When the ear begins to hear, and the eye begins to see;
When the pulse begins to throb—the brain to think again—
The soul to feel the flesh, and the flesh to feel the chain.
Yet I would lose no sting, would wish no torture less,
The more that anguish racks, the earlier it will bless;
And robed in fires of hell, or bright with heavenly shine,
If it but herald Death, the vision is divine.

Who else in England was thinking that straight? But generations had to be born, and die, to give place to other generations, before her poetry was recognized as great.

In a life so purposefully obscure one cannot but wonder at the love poems.

Cold in the earth—and fifteen wild Decembers
    From those brown hills have melted into spring:
Faithful, indeed, is the spirit that remembers
    After such years of change and suffering!

Sweet Love of youth, forgive, if I forget thee,
    While the world's tide is bearing me along;
Other desires and other hopes beset me,
    Hopes which obscure, but cannot do thee wrong!

No later light has lightened up my heaven,
    No second morn has ever shone for me;
All my life's bliss from thy dear life was given,
    All my life's bliss is in the grave with thee.

And, even yet, I dare not let it languish,
    Dare not indulge in memory's rapturous pain;
Once drinking deep of that divinest anguish
    How could I seek the empty world again?

All this may be imaginary, but again, it may confess an early trouble which, till death, fed her soul and therefore her writing. Fifteen, one muses. But a number may be arbitrary; it may even be put there deliberately to mislead. The lines are convincing, they do not sound like a girl who has had no experience of painful love.

Her sardonic novel *Wuthering Heights*—"the action of which," Dante Gabriel Rossetti said, "is laid in hell, only it seems places and people have English names there"—was finally published, but instead of churning up the entire millpond made only a little ripple, moving outward. One of the few great novels of the world hardly wrinkled the glassy surface; and this when Charlotte's *Jane Eyre,* incalculably inferior, was being talked about all over literary England. Emily flung out on the moors. Charlotte's praise must have pricked, if it held the note of condescension one distinguishes in her preface to the new edition, after Emily's death: "Heathcliff, indeed," says Charlotte, "stands unredeemed. . . . Whether it is right or advisable to create beings like Heathcliff, I do not know: I scarcely think it is." She did not see that Heathcliff exemplifies the warping of an individual by cruel early environment; that the redemption of his prototype Hareton by the warm love of the second Catherine is vicarious redemption, not only for Heathcliff but the Catherine who lay in her grave; indeed, that Heathcliff's evil is self-doomed and self-destroyed. Terror, but some pity too, informs the story. Mr. Lockwood seizes the cold hands of Cathy's ghost through the window sash, and when she cries to be taken in after twenty years and will not let go, rubs her wrists back and forth on the broken glass; and then Heathcliff stark awake sobs, "Come in! come in! Cathy, do come. Oh do come—*once* more!" And, later, Cathy tears the pillow with her teeth and pulls out the feathers, ranging them on the sheet,

"That's a turkey's, and this is a wild duck's; and this is a pigeon's. Ah, they put pigeons' feathers in the pillows— no wonder I couldn't die. . . ."

She defies the husband she has never loved for the man she could never help loving,

"Hush! Hush, this moment! You mention that name and I end the matter instantly, by a spring from the window! What you touch at present you may have; but my soul will be on that hill-top before you lay hands on me again."

And in that peace-destroying final interview between Cathy and Heathcliff, washed by each other's tears, Cathy entreats him, "If I've done wrong, I'm dying for it. I forgive you. Forgive me!"

One simply cannot stop reading *Wuthering Heights,* not for anything, for anything else seems unimportant. The very weather has significance beyond what we know as weather.

"All that remained of the day was a beamless amber light along the west: but I could see every pebble on the path, and every blade of grass, by that splendid moon."

119

And,

"In the evening, the weather broke; the wind shifted from south to north-east, and brought rain first, and then sleet and snow. On the morrow one could hardly imagine that there had been three weeks of summer: the primroses and crocuses were hidden under wintry drifts; the larks were silent, the young leaves of the early trees smitten and blackened."

Cathy says,

"And that wind sounding in the firs by the lattice. Do let me feel it—it comes straight down the moor—do let me have one breath. . . . Oh, I'm burning! I wish I were out of doors! I wish I were a girl again, half savage, and hardy, and free. . . . Open the window wide: fasten it open!"

This is Emily—the very Emily—austere and ecstatic.

When Charlotte read aloud a typical stupid criticism of *Wuthering Heights,* which spoke of "Ellis Bell" the author as "a man of uncommon talents, but dogged, brutal and morose," Emily smiled faintly.

It was December, 1848, and at Branwell's funeral, in November, Emily had caught a bad cold. She was thirty.

For weeks she breathed in short, irregular gasps, and toiled up the stone stairs step by step, leaning against the cold wall for support, but never complaining, and with white face so stern her sisters dared not follow nor offer help. She would have "no poisoning doctor," she said. The only possible conclusion is that she more than yielded to darkness: she invited it and courted it.

Charlotte, who knew now how much she loved Emily, searched the barren moors for heather, and found in a hollow a withered spray; but Emily was already so withdrawn from this world she could not recognize the familiar flower.

The last day of her life she insisted on dressing herself without aid, though will-power could no longer keep her from staggering, and her eyes glazed.

Unwarmed, she sat by the fire, combing slowly her dark hair—slowly, slowly, the long dark hair. When the comb slipped from her grasp she could not stoop to pick it up. They found it on the floor, later.

IX

CHARLOTTE BRONTË

IT would be easy for those who love Emily Brontë to resent her sister Charlotte; but it would not be fair.

Charlotte's life, in outward circumstances, parallelled Emily's life, except that Charlotte was longer at Miss Wooler's School and the Héger Pensionnat, had a fuller experience as a governess, was, made love to, and lived to see herself a successful novelist. Their heredity was the same, their childhoods almost identical. Even their deaths had similarities. But as human beings they were almost opposites. The Reverend Patrick Brontë and *le professeur* Constantin Héger were right in crediting Emily with genius and Charlotte, at best, with great talent.

But the real difference went much deeper. However meekly Emily did the family ironing and swept the parlour carpet, she was, in her heart always, as on the moors, the wild one, the sensitive one, the one altogether audacious and not to be caught or predicted.

Charlotte was a congenital spinster. On the moors, in childhood, she had been one of five spinsters, all under ten. Maria and Elizabeth died, as a solution. Emily and Anne put dying off a little while, to become, first, free and unprecise. But as Charlotte had begun, she ended: there was something tenacious about her always. As a small knowing spinster "clever of her age" she started to school, and thereafter till she died piously picked up knowledge. She was a spinster by fate and by habit: shy, nervous, stubborn, near-sighted, with her book pushed up to her nose, proper under stress, dutiful and righteous.

When her mother and her motherly sister Maria died, Charlotte was forced, by circumstances now as well as temperament, to manage. Aunt Elizabeth Branwell's arrival only postponed her stewardship. The discipline at the miserable school at Cowan Bridge and the sometimes humiliating subordination of a governess in private homes seemed to aggravate an innate love of setting in order, like needles and thread in a workbasket, her own and other people's affairs. By dint of a little duplicity and well-calculated maneuvering she got herself and Emily sent to the young ladies' school in Brussels. Here, as at Roe Head, Emily's cry was for freedom. What did Charlotte care about freedom? She did quite well without the moors. The world was not too much with her, late and soon, getting and spending. She wanted the world; but wanted it arranged and tidy, like an orthodox spinster's top drawer. She wrote admirable prose, but her poetry was poor.

Spinsters in the psychological sense, like spinsters in the physical, are apt to be prudes. The granddaughter of an Irish peasant named Prunty, Charlotte criticized as of low extraction her employers the Whites. Well could she believe that Mrs. White was only an exciseman's daughter. The high-flown, haughty fancies of the Brontë children had been practiced so long that Charlotte had come to believe them. Pride is a recurrent note in the novels, *Jane Eyre, Shirley,* and *Villette,* which set London agog. She still seems to be saying, though by proxy, "I am the Duke of Wellington!"

But she was never really at ease in a larger world than Haworth, being "weighed down and oppressed by a miserable *mauvaise honte";* and frightened and therefore dull, as at Thackeray's party in London. One of the guests asked the honour-guest, the brilliant Currer Bell: "Do you like London?" Miss Brontë did not relax. There was a decorous silence; a pause. "Yes," she said, "and no."

Three curates sued for her hand: the Reverend Henry Nussey, her friend Ellen's brother; the Irish Reverend Bryce, "witty—lively—ardent—clever too"; and the straight-laced, ponderous Reverend Arthur Bell Nicholls. Although in *Shirley* she had damned all curates as "a self-seeking, vain and empty race," as a last resort she married Mr. Nicholls. Whether her infatuation for M. Héger of the Héger Pensionnat in Brussels was dead or alive in her breast the day of the wedding, we can only conjecture. We know that when M. Héger warned her that his wife disapproved of her letters and suggested a secret address, she was horrified and broke off. The whole of her life had been a testimony to the proprieties. Whatever her heart, her will was stern undeviating law. True, after her father's angry dismissal of Mr. Nicholls, his curate, for having had the temerity to court her, she carried on a correspondence *sub rosa*. But Mr. Nicholls was not married; and soon she repented and confessed. When at last she persuaded her father to consent (though he refused to attend the wedding) did she do it because she was lonely and bored? But it turned out that the conjugal state suited her very well. Hearing, at the end, after nine month's of married life, her husband's prayer that God spare her, "Oh!" she whispered, "I am not going to die, am I? He will not separate us, we have been so happy."

Even spinsters dream of passion. In her novels Charlotte Brontë, gifted with the power of minute observation and a prodigious memory, juggled time and disguised names, but one hears in the fervent accents of Jane Eyre, Caroline Helstone and Lucy Snowe the voice of Charlotte herself, hunting for a dark hero of Byronic cast of feature. "Her heroines," wrote Harriet Martineau, "love too readily, too vehemently . . ." and turned resolutely away from the "morbid in passion." Such writing was a spinster's compensation. In Charlotte's last illness the servant Martha Brown tried to cheer her with the thought of the baby coming, but she was not cheered. The spinster had not dreamed of a baby.

Branwell, her childhood ally and collaborator, had died, unforgiven for his affair with a married woman, and for drinking, and drug-taking. He had been a waste, and she could not bear wastes. Emily had died unconverted to her sister's sensible viewpoint, and was now only grudgingly acknowledged as glorious. Violet-eyed Anne had died, in a sense unknown, though mourned. Papa, with his pistol-shooting habits and monstrous cravat, like Tithonus would never die.

It was her turn to make a good job of death. So many were watching to see how she would do it: Miss Martineau with whom she had quarrelled over an adverse criticism of *Villette;* Mr. Thackeray who hung on the parlour wall with the Duke of Wellington; Mrs. Gaskell, her competent future biographer; Ellen Nussey, her lifelong confidante, undistinguished, but of solid virtues compact; Haworth villagers whom she had taught in the Sunday School, and passed, with a nod, on the slippery cobbled hill; and that shadowy sea of faces which her publisher called her public. The thirty-nine allotted years (1816-1855) were up. Weak from an obscure disorder of the stomach, she went into a low delirium, begging for the food which for days she had refused, and even for stimulants. A consciousness of absolute integrity comforted her, but not for everything.

Imagination can conjure up a pale dying Charlotte Brontë, dress her in a discreet high-necked cotton night-gown, braid her thick brown hair in pigtails, and set her hands straight. But we cannot be sure about the features of her face. A few weeks before her death, she had written Ellen Nussey about her illness, adding, "I am rather mortified to lose my good looks. . . ." That is strange, for never had she been credited with good looks. In our confusion we examine her portraits, and find them as contradictory as her life was paradoxical. Branwell's painting gives her, at eighteen, a jowled, hard look unlike the well-bred intellectual woman Richmond painted. Is the Richmond portrait shameless flattery? Old Mr. Brontë, while complaining that it looked older than his daughter, declared that the countenance was faithful in feature, and the expression "wonderfully good and life-like." The brow is high, broad, and clear, the cheek-modelling sensitive, the eyes thoughtful and rather beautiful. But the lower lip, as Branwell noted, protrudes, and the nose hooks slightly and is disproportionately large. To focus the whole, one must remember that, although Harriet Martineau was wrong in saying that Charlotte, due to hunger, never grew an inch after Cowan Bridge, she was an elfin-sized creature, smaller and in certain ways more dynamic than any of her sisters.

The stone-floored parlour which let on to a dank, disease-laden graveyard had been the scene of fierce struggles and dismal events. Here the three sisters had written their novels; here Emily had been "torn, conscious, panting" from life; here the curious had come to gape at the famous and been served at a table exquisitely clean, neat, and simple. Here, when none were left but Charlotte and her father, the long hours passed slowly to the ticking of the clock in the kitchen, and the buzzing of a fly on the outside of the pane. All was grey without, and now, with the working of time, all was grey within. Did Charlotte, in the gloom, recognize her fit and proper hàbitation? Was she glad that now she could keep a chair from being pushed an inch out of place, and could spirit a cluttering pencil or a guilty handkerchief out of sight the minute it was dropped?

Years ago, in a vivid and typical passage in *Jane Eyre,* she had described Rochester's drawing-room at Thornfield, and it is evident that this again was a spinster's subconscious rebellion against drab monotony:

"She pointed to a wide arch corresponding to the window, and hung like it with a Tyrian-dyed curtain, now looped up. Mounting to it by two broad steps, and looking through, I thought I caught a glimpse of a fairy place, so bright to my novice eyes appeared the view beyond. Yet it was merely a very pretty drawing room, and within it a boudoir, both spread with white carpets, on which seemed laid brilliant garlands of flowers; both ceiled with snowy mouldings of white grapes and vine-leaves, beneath which glowed in rich contrast crimson couches and ottomans; while the ornaments on the pale Parian mantelpiece were of sparkling Bohemian glass, ruby red, and between the windows large mirrors repeated the general blending of snow and fire."

Charlotte Brontë surveyed the parsonage parlour ruefully. All that she saw was in good taste, but the total effect was bare and cold and grey, like the moors. She thought of her father's fanatical fear of fire and lifelong stricture against curtains of any kind. But she resolved to overrule him. Every melancholy window should have its crimson denial; the old sofa and every dull chair, its bright defense. That day she was happy.

And that day, as every other day of her life, "being constructed on a perfectly comprehensible plan," she was not, in spite of troubles and the menace of an early death, a tragic character. She was an uncommonly good writer, but she was not quite big enough in her soul to be tragic.

X

SAINT TERESA

Saint Teresa died at sixty-seven and from her tomb, it was said, exuded the odor of violets.

This phenomenon, if true, is not more wonderful than a mind putting together words in such a way that intense experience is clearly communicated. It is power of expression without falsification which places Saint Teresa among the distinguished women writers of the world, whatever her status in the Church. Her *Autobiography,* as the history of a soul engaged in sloughing off this mortal coil, is comparable to the *Confessions* of St. Augustine. Her *The Way of Perfection, The Book of the Foundations, The Interior Castle,* and letters are, as prose, sound and straightforward and beautiful. There are poems too, stung with ecstasy.

> Living, in me I do not live
> Because my hope is set so high:
> Dying, I do not die.

Many have prayed for fame, but this woman for nonentity. When at forty-six she was commanded by her Confessor to write the story of her life, she obeyed as if it were a penance, protesting that only with God's help could she do it, for she was ignorant. The manuscript was left as it was written first, uncorrected and unpolished.

"I had not finished perusing it," she said, "when Your Reverence sent for it; hence some things are not mentioned as they should be, and others I may have repeated."

If Father Avila was to censure it, she begged that it be transcribed—"otherwise someone might know the hand."

The facts of years of meditation are almost lost, in any life—indeed in such years vision becomes the only truth: eating and drinking and dressing and going to bed are the illusions.

She was born in 1515 in Avila, old Castile, of the noble house of Cepeda. Her father, though wealthy, was too compassionate to keep slaves; her mother, though beautiful in the lush incredible Spanish way, "made no account of it." At six or seven (she declares that as a child she was wicked) she began to be troubled by books on the sacraments and by her mother's devout religious observances. She and one of her nine brothers read the *Lives of the Saints,* and started off to trudge to the land where the Moors were, begging their way for the love of God, for the express purpose of being put to death. When their parents captured them and dragged them home, the thwarted martyrs built hermitages in the garden—but the stones fell down. So there was nothing to do but play convent, at an age when unsanctimonious children play blindman's bluff and hide-and-go-seek.

But her "wicked" strain came out again when she commenced to read books on knight-errantry. She "confesses" that if she could not obtain new books she was miserable. Of a sudden it seemed very important to dazzle people with fine clothes, and she lavished great care on hands and tresses, and was extravagantly fond of perfume. But her "worst menace" was conversations with certain cousins-german who were visiting her father's house, and one in particular; which so changed her, she says, that "there remained scarcely any sign of my former good disposition." What were these corrupting conversations? Her Confessor forbade her to expatiate upon her sins, so we are told only that they were "about a marriage."

At fourteen, while being educated in a convent at Avila, she came under the influence of "a very holy nun," but the whole history of Christ's passion, she says, could not draw a single tear from her eye. She did not want to become a sister, but was afraid to marry; she had at that time scarcely an intimation of "how great was the vanity of the world," which "would shortly end." When at last she took the brown habit of the Carmelite Convent of the Incarnation, with the white mantle over it, she was actuated, she says, by fear rather than love.

And then, though she was not yet twenty, her health failed: she had fainting fits and was all but burned up by fever. The cures of terrible afflictions, in those days, were as violent as the diseases; but she endured all with resignation, and for three years read the Book of Job;

at the end of which time she fell into a four-day trance. Extreme Unction was administered, and they dug her grave, and dropped candle-wax on her eyes. When she revived, she was carried to the convent in a sheet, for she could not bear the touch of hands. Then she applied to heavenly physicians, as she puts it, and took Saint Joseph as her patron, and before long could walk.

But now, she says, she succumbed to "new vanities," hinted at but not described, for which she blames youth, sensuality and the devil. Further "conversations" with someone for whom she "felt too much affection" made her break off praying, for in her heart she had a conviction of unworthiness. Then her father died, and his Dominican Confessor spoke to her gravely. Thereafter, though much tempted, she abhorred "the amusements of this world." But without the good priest's help, she says, she "would still be going on, falling and rising, till I had fallen headlong into hell."

Her "rising" she compares to the flight of a little bird, and the figure, pleasing her, is used again and again. As her spirit grew with contemplation, the little bird became an eagle of "quick and strong impetuosity"; she learned to hazard everything, to abandon her soul to God.

The four degrees of prayer, which is spiritual abandonment, she explains patiently in *The Way of Perfection*.

Whoever begins prayer, she says, should imagine he

is planting a garden, for the delight of the Lord, in unfruitful soil choked with weeds; and should water the tender shoots, lest they bring forth no sweet-smelling flowers, but withered. A garden may be watered in four different ways: first, by "drawing water out of a well," the difficult first strivings; second, by using "a wheel with buckets attached to it"—the "prayer of quiet" in which the soul "recollects within herself all her faculties and has nothing to do but enjoy her sweetness without making any noise"; third, by "letting some small stream run into the garden"—the "prayer of union" in which the soul is engulfed in grace, "as when a person is on the point of dying the death he desires, with a blessed candle in his hands"; or fourth, by "a good shower of rain, for then the Lord Himself waters the garden."

Sister Teresa, who prayed so much, began to fall into strange raptures. Her visions seem to have been of the same species as the angels which William Blake saw clustered in a tree, and the prophets strolling in the evening air—and he always stoutly maintained that they were, not hallucinations, but real celestial entities. The nun Teresa says that once the Lord picked up the cross on her rosary and returned it studded with four great stones more precious than diamonds, but visible only to her eyes. And once an angel, "not tall, but rather little, and very beautiful," pierced her heart with a long golden dart pointed and winged with fire. When she saw a bad spirit or devil, she says, she threw Holy Water and routed him, and for this Christ spoke to her "with His most lovely and divine mouth." But when, from curiosity, she tried to see the colour and largeness and shape of his eyes, she "could not gain my object by any diligence."

But are not poets always pierced in the side by light? A poet is a state of mind. Saint Teresa had the state of mind. When she spoke or wrote, her thoughts were shiningly communicated, but usually the state of mind was inarticulate, or triumphed in a burning act, to prove that poetry and rhapsodic religion converge. Indeed one of her works proved it so gloriously that she was almost caught in the toils of the Inquisition.

She was past forty when she felt an imperative urge and founded a stricter order, Saint Joseph's. Spain, reinforced by the whole of Christendom, marshalled against her, and she was slandered, persecuted and laughed at. But serenely she went about her difficult task, and without revenue, or hope of any, banded together thirteen nuns, who took a vow of poverty, ate no flesh, fasted eight months a year, and walked in sandals. To Teresa even her reformed order was not severe enough, and she wore under the brown habit a peculiarly painful hairshirt. And at last those who had scoffed, gave alms.

After the Convent at Avila, where she spent five years, Teresa founded, among others, the Convents of

Medina del Campo, Malagon, Toledo, Salamanca, Segovia, Veas, and Sevilla—seventeen convents and sixteen monasteries in all.

But leaving Burgos, the last and most trying, for Avila, in 1582, she felt "an incredible decay of strength." Nothing, at the moment, could be found for her but a few dry figs. After some vicissitudes she was put to bed in the house of the Duchess of Alva, and fell to praying. When her Confessor told her to entreat the Lord not to take her so soon, she replied that she was no longer useful in this world. Though stiff with pain, as soon as the Pledge of Redemption was brought she sat up in bed with vigour and ease, as if suddenly well, and her face shone. "The hour I have long wished for," she said, "is now come." She went into an ecstasy, holding her cross tightly. When they touched her she was dead.

Only a life which stands still can stagnate. Only the indifference which is "dryness of soul" can shut out higher truth. Ignorant of Latin and hence, for the most part, of the Breviary, Teresa, whom the Church has made a saint, speaks with the dignity of the learned. One may accept literally or figuratively certain of her descriptions, as when she speaks of being lifted bodily from the floor, in ecstasy, or of being shown the place prepared for her in hell before her conversion, or of being addressed by God, without voice but in sentences which could be parsed. Her sincerity cannot be doubted. One hears the true, unfeigned, indisputable accent. She anticipates accusers and condemners, for they were bound to arise, by having no mercy on herself. Is vision merely an illusion born of arrogance? she asks, and decides that she has never been guilty of arrogance, but only, in youth, of false humility, which is troublesome, compared to genuine humility,

"which comes not with any disorder, nor does it disturb the soul, nor overcloud her, nor cause in her any aridity, but rather comforts her, and proceeds otherwise, with gentleness, sweetness and delight."

How close are religion and art. Both cry for spiritual beauty, and both must learn to be humble, to forget self, in order to reflect clearly, like a mirror unblemished by a particle of dust. If Teresa's vehement spirit had turned to art instead of religion, it would have found a different but related medium and pleasure. In the brightness of the soul's heat all is welded. When she remembers intensely what was intensely experienced, the metaphors crowd thick, fast, rich and sure—as when she says that the weakness of Peter of Alcantara was so extreme "he seems made only of the roots of trees"; and likens the light in visions to

"pure water running over crystal, the sun reflecting it and striking through it, in contradistinction to muddy water, seen on a cloudy day, and running upon an earthy bottom";

and speaks of that desirable love which

"should be collected within, and not, like a kettle, suffered to boil over because wood has been piled on the fire without discretion."

The rightness of this Spanish nun's language survives even faulty translation—which should have been at once substantial, forthright and lyrical, like the King James Version of the Bible.

For Saint Teresa's life was lyrical, whether or not this was a factor in her canonization. Her visions are symbols and spiritual dramatizations, like those in primitive painting. Any poet understands them instinctively, and is moved.

XI

EMILY DICKINSON

On a white slip of paper Emily Dickinson once wrote, "Area—no test of depth," and sent it with a gift to a friend. It is the truest, the most piercing, the only perfect comment on a singular life.

Her "area" was for a time the small precise town of Amherst, Massachusetts, where she was born in 1830. Then, after school days, it shrank to the garden which enclosed her father's house.

Did she draw an invisible line and refuse to step across it because of an oath made in pique; or a desire to symbolize difference of soul by difference of conduct; or because, having taken the "immortal wound" and renounced the beloved inflictor, she felt contempt for or indifference to the world, her life being elsewhere, within? These questions have been asked but not answered. We only know that a tireless and measureless probing inward, since she could not, or would not, expand outward, is recorded in poems as limited in size as her backyard, and yet, like her mind, of "colossal substance."

Mabel Loomis Todd had long been acquainted with Lavinia the sister and Austin the brother when she met Emily the recluse, then fifty years old. But what an odd meeting. Evening after evening Mrs. Todd sat at the square piano in the stiff, uncomfortable Dickinson drawing-room, playing Beethoven, Scarlatti, Chopin,

Haydn, Bach, while outside, in the dusk-dark hall, crouched a diminutive white figure, transported by hearing classical composers for the first time. At the end of the concert Maggie the maid was sent in with the listener's gratitude: a glass of wine on a silver tray, a piece of cake or a fresh-picked long-stemmed rose, and perhaps a scrap of paper on which was written, shyly, a poem.

Emily has not yet come out of the twilit hall. We have her poems, most of her letters, and the reminiscences of a few who heard her speak and even saw her. But the numerous solutions of her mystery remain to be solved. "Biography," said Emily Dickinson, "first convinces me of the fleeing of the biographied."

With every fact known, genius can no more be arrested and scrutinized face to face than a phantom.

A few facts about the head and moving force of the Dickinson household are known:

On Sunday Mr. Dickinson, lawyer, read "lonely and rigorous books"; he would eat Emily's bread and no one else's; he insisted on giving medicine, especially if the patient rebelled; he would not admit that he enjoyed Jenny Lind's singing; he refrained from kissing his children; when Emily at thirty-six had to go to a Boston eye-specialist, he objected, on the ground that he was "in the habit of her"; he forbade her to marry, and when, just once, she questioned his authority, he put on his great cape and his high beaver hat, grasped his gold-headed cane, tapped the floor hard—and the matter was settled for another thirty years. But he cracked nuts with his family, after supper; and requested his daughter Emily to perform the "Lancers' Quickstep" on the piano; and when, his last afternoon on earth, though with no premonition, she preferred his company and made an excuse to leave her mother, he said as the June light waned, "I would like it not to end. . . ."

A few facts about Emily's education, also, are known:

At Amherst Academy, at fourteen, she studied Botany, Geology, Latin and Mental Philosophy; at South Hadley Female Seminary, at sixteen, Algebra, Euclid and Ecclesiastical History. She read *Evangeline, The Princess, The Maiden Aunt*. She slowly approached Keats, the Brownings, Ruskin, Sir Thomas Browne, and St. John's *Revelations*. At forty she said of Shakespeare, "Why is any other book needed?"

But what goes into a head as education does not explain what comes out of it in fierce originality.

And her heart, since a poet without a heart never lived?

When she was twenty a young schoolmaster named Leonard Humphrey died. A week before his death he had written her, while in perfect health, that he would die and that she would become a poet. Ten years after his death she said:

"When a little girl, I had a friend who taught me Immortality, but venturing too near himself, never returned. Soon after, my tutor died, and for several years my lexicon was my only companion. Then I found one more, but he was not contented I be his scholar, so he left the land."

The literary world has been trying for years to discover the name of this "one more." Was he George Gould?—a tall spiritual-eyed, full-lipped young scholar, brilliant at Amherst and the Union Theological Seminary, who was frowned on by her father because of poverty, and did indeed, for two years, "leave the land." Was he Major Edward Hunt?—Helen Hunt Jackson's first husband, who was killed at thirty-two while experimenting with an invention, and who, Emily once remarked, "interested me more than any man I ever saw." Was it the Reverend Doctor Charles Wadsworth?—a married Philadelphia minister, whom her father introduced to her when she was twenty-three and he forty, on the fatal five-weeks trip to Washington and Philadelphia which ended with her retirement from the world. Dr. Wadsworth and Miss Dickinson corresponded, and he may have come to see her more than once, for she said that the last time he came "in life" she asked, "How long?"—meaning, since they had met—and he answered, "with inscrutable roguery," "Twenty years."

These are all facts, but they do not "split the lark and find the music, bulb after bulb in silver rolled . . ."

That she loved a man and of her own volition relinquished him is of great importance in understanding her character and her poetry.   But does it matter whom she gave her heart to, and lost?   If tomorrow it were proved beyond the possibility of doubt that the man her soul fixed upon was George Gould, or Charles Wadsworth, or a man never before mentioned, curiosity would cease —that is all.   Great poetry, when most personal, transcends personality: it soars out of the realm of names.

> So we must keep apart,
> You there, I here,
> With just the door ajar
> That oceans are,
> And prayer,
> And that pale sustenance,
> Despair!

That she continued to love the man is certain.   "Mine by the right of white election!"   "He put the belt around my life,—I heard the buckle snap."   "Empty my heart of thee, its single artery?"   "Alter? When the hills do." Days, and weeks, and years went by, but

> To fill a gap—
> Insert the thing that caused it.
> Block it up
> With other and 'twill yawn
> The more;
> You cannot solder an abyss
> With air.

She wore clean piqué dresses, white, like a pledge of faith, till the day of her death.

The world feels dusty
When we stop to die;
We want the dew then,
Honors taste dry.

Flags vex a dying face,
But the least fan
Stirred by a friend's hand
Cools like the rain.

Mine be the ministry
When thy thirst comes,
Dews of thyself to fetch
And holy balms.

But it would be a misemphasis to make a tragedy out of a solitary, but not an idle, life. "Near yet remote," she cultivated a few people as carefully as her flowers. Mrs. Dickinson "did not care for thought"; Mr. Dickinson was "too busy with his briefs to notice what they did"; but there was plain, sharp, loyal sister Lavinia, who tried on Emily's white dresses, by proxy, to spare her the dressmaker, addressed Emily's envelopes, to spare her the public's eyes, and stirred up Emily's pudding when she lingered in her room, mysteriously occupied; and next door there was her brother Austin's wife, "Sister Sue," to whom she could show the poems which came out of her deepest self, for Sue, being in her own way audacious, understood audacity.

Letters were to Emily the doorbell she could answer, who answered none, the hand she could take, who took none, the face she could see in the full light of lamps, who saw none, in her later years, to decipher. "A letter feels to me like immortality," she said, "because it is the mind alone without corporeal friend"—and here, as often, the lines of her prose can be scanned.

If friends like Dr. and Mrs. Holland or Mr. and Mrs. Bowles lapsed in their correspondence, she scourged them with loving words:

"I write to you. I receive no letter. I say 'they dignify my trust.' I do not disbelieve. . . . My business is to love. I found a bird this morning, down—down—on a little bush at the foot of the garden, and wherefore sing, I said, since nobody *hears*. One sob in the throat, one flutter of bosom —'*My* business is to *sing*'—and away she rose!"

In a silence broken only by letters which sometimes did not come, and the *Springfield Republican,* minute events were, naturally, magnified as under a microscope. Half a dozen frozen birds collapsed on the kitchen sill; Carlo her "shaggy ally" barked at a shadow; she made a hood for Vinnie; "two butterflies went out at noon and waltzed above a stream, then stepped straight through the firmament. . . ." Weather was dispensation or catastrophe: "An awful tempest mashed the air." "The moon was but a chin of gold." "A drop fell on the orchard." In the garden she crumbled clods, and weeded, and sprinkled, and watched the buds swell, squatting, on wet days, on an old red frayed-out rug.

The murmur of a bee
A witchcraft yieldeth me.
If any ask me why,
'Twere easier to die
Than tell.

The red upon the hill
Taketh away my will.
. . . .
The breaking of the day
Addeth to my degree . . . .

And,

I tend my flowers for thee,
Bright Absentee!
My fuchsia's coral seams
Rip, while the sower dreams . . . .

She dreamed till she was thirty, and then began
to write poems. Was it the crystallizing power of the
Civil War, which she lived through, or simply that by
thirty she had reached (and would have reached, in any
circumstances) spiritual maturity? Leonard Humphrey
had declared with the prescience of the about-to-die
that she would be a poet, and suddenly it seemed that she
was. But how could she be certain? In the spring of
her thirty-second year she wrote Thomas Wentworth
Higginson, one of the literary arbiters of her day,

"Are you too deeply occupied to say if my verse is alive?
The mind is so near itself it cannot see distinctly, and I have
none to ask,"

and enclosed four poems. Colonel Higginson's first letter may be imagined from her quick "Thank you for the surgery, it was not so painful as I supposed," and the pertness, yet inviolate innocence, of her prompt answers to his questions about her age, books, training, companion, family and whether or not she had read Whitman (she had not). A photograph?

"Could you believe me without? I have no portrait, now, but am small, like the wren; and my hair is bold, like the chestnut burr; and my eyes, like the sherry in the glass that the guest leaves."

Thus began an instruction during which the rôles of pupil and teacher were reversed.

If Colonel Higginson was a bit chary of his praise, it is not surprising, for the appearance of an important woman poet was, in the light of history, extremely improbable, and required special discernment to see and bravery to hail. There have been comparatively few women poets. The *Oxford Book of English Verse,* a balanced and just anthology, gives space to twenty-four women as opposed to two hundred and forty-four men, and many of the twenty-four are represented by one easily forgotten lyric. Women, in general, seem deficient in the distinguishing talents of the great poets: they are not dramatic, nor philosophic, nor epic; they do not look far back nor far forward in time; they are more or less indifferent to "real existence," an eager desire for the knowledge of which Plato postulated as the first requirement of the true philosophic disposition; they seem unable to synthesize many small confusing facts into one divinely simple fact; their eyes stab upward and downward, shallowly, neglecting the cosmos. But though—with the exception of Sappho—they must be denied membership in that band of poets who perceive like gods, mighty and select affiliation which includes Homer, and Lucretius, and Virgil, and Dante, and the author of *The Song of Roland,* and Shakespeare, and Goethe, and Milton and Blake, nevertheless eight or ten women form a group that is near-great, or great in all but the first sense. Still, how was Colonel Higginson to guess the species of the bird the wind had blown against his door? The lady was so thoroughly a woman, and it is doubtful whether he had spent much time meditating on the fact that in poetry a woman's success, as in life a woman's destiny, does not consist in being other than she is: she is an individual before she is a woman, but must develop along her own lines if she is to develop at all. Colonel Higginson was looking for a certain thing, and finding another, did not see it clearly and completely, for what it was. But he was polite; he was gallant; he did not tell her to go back to her bread-baking. Those intimate fierce thoughts set down in dubious rhyme stuck in his memory.

Eight years went by, and then one day genial Colonel Higginson walked up to a fine old red brick house in

Amherst and had an interview with Miss Emily Dickinson—"a remarkable experience," he wrote his wife, "quite equalling my expectations," and went on to relate how she "glided in," dressed in spotless white, "a little plain woman with two smooth bands of reddish hair." Her voice was timid, but once she had begun, she talked without difficulty.

"How do most people live without any thoughts?" she said. "There are many people in the world (you must have noticed them in the street), how do they live? How do they get strength to put on their clothes in the morning?"

And, "I find ecstasy in living; the mere *sense* of living is joy enough." And,

"If I read a book and it makes my whole body so cold no fire can warm me, I know *that* is poetry. If I feel physically as if the top of my head were taken off, I know *that* is poetry. These are the only ways I know it. Is there any other way?"

Mr. Higginson said later that no one had ever drained his nerve power so much; that without touching him she drew from him, and he was glad he did not live near her.

During the next fifteen years her pile of poems grew like something animate. There was enough high explosive in her drawer to have wrecked the red-brick mansion, and demolished the block. But all along the street, under the great outspreading pines, it was unspeakably quiet.

Presentiment is that long shadow on the lawn
Indicative that suns go down;
The notice to the startled grass
That darkness is about to pass.

Her father died first, leaving her desolate and aghast. One cannot study the lives of outstanding women, and especially of outstanding women poets, without noticing the profound influence of fathers upon daughters—which is significant. Of Emily Brontë with her forbidding father, and Christina Rossetti with her fiery academic one, and Alice Meynell with her gentlemanly one, and Elizabeth Barrett Browning with her thunderous one, and Emily Dickinson with her legal and adored one, it might be said, as Dryden said of Lady Ann Killigrew, "Thy father was transfused into thy blood."

After her father, Mr. Bowles died, and then Dr. Holland, and then, as a climax to years of paralysis, her mother, and then the Reverend Charles Wadsworth, and then her dear eight-year-old nephew Gilbert, next door. As the result of too much contemplation of death, or something else, she was plunged into an enigmatical mental darkness, which she fought, and in time won her way out of, only to sink again, at fifty-five, with Bright's disease.

The heart asks pleasure first;
And then, excuse from pain;
And then those little anodynes
That deaden suffering.

> And then, to go to sleep;
> And then, if it should be
> The will of the Inquisitor,
> The liberty to die.

She had been in bed for months, and was just beginning to creep around, an hour a day, when something insisted, and she wrote one of her characteristically short notes to the children who played under her window: "Little Cousins—Called Back."

Thus passed from the obscurity of her life to the obscurity of death perhaps the greatest American poet, irrespective of sex. The technical irregularities of her verse are, for the most part, not flaws but a forecast. Whether she wrote of the immensities of time, love, pain, justice, hope or death, or the minutiae of her garden—a robin, a snake, a mushroom, a berry, a clover, a bee—the words strike through, sharply, to the ultimate and incorruptible. Hardly anything escaped the scrutiny of her great brown eyes. Occasional coyness is easily forgiven this spinster, this gnome, this keeper-of-faith, this demure wrestler-with-God. Since she stands so securely among the poets of the world, stanchly New-England in the white piqué, her own poem is her best praise:

> I reckon, when I count at all,
> First Poets—then the Sun—
> Then Summer—then the
> Heaven of God—
> And then the list is done.

> But looking back—the first so seems
> To comprehend the whole—
> The others look a needless show,
> So I write Poets—All.

When Mr. Higginson went to Amherst the last time, in 1886, he found his "scholar" looking wonderfully young—nearer thirty than fifty-five. Vinnie had put into her cold hand two heliotropes, and tied a knot of violets at her pulseless throat, and one long pale cypripedium. Silently Emily went from her father's house; silently down the street. People were milling about, some of them utter strangers. She did not mind, now. The fate of the hundreds of unpublished poems did not trouble her. "If fame belonged to me," she had said once, quietly, "I could not escape her." Meanwhile there was the immortality Father had recommended.

XII

ALICE MEYNELL

Alice Meynell had exceptional endowments in a richly endowed generation, but not genius. That gap, that faint defect, that unfortunate falling short, which it seems ungenerous to mention, what was it? We read her exquisitely reserved essays, her disciplined poetry, and the ardent praise of her contemporaries, yet return stubbornly to our disappointment. Until we know its cause we are fascinated by deficiency. It is not so much a passion for blaming as for understanding. The mind or the heart, which failed?

Her mind, though not bold in speculation, nor wide-ranging, was a fastidious, sane and vigilant labourer in small plots. She pulled up weeds, straightened rows, had the right touch with graceful, less known, delicate plants—"yonder handful of long sedges and rushes in a vase." She arranged them with taste, in a showery spray, so that they cast lovely grey shadows on a pale surface of wall.

Having defended the mind must we accuse the heart? Was there a fissure in the crystal?

No, the heart that loved England where she was born, and Italy where she spent most of her childhood, and her scholarly father, and her gifted mother, and the Catholic Church to which she was converted at twenty, and her husband, and her eight children, and a multitude of friends, and found time to love, unfeignedly, all the aspects of a changing world, was a large heart, and a good one, without blemish.

Then was she too civilized for breathless evocation?

From her birth in 1850 to her death in 1923, her life was correct, punctilious and well-bred. She was attached to pleasant things, and devoted to everlasting ones, and did not overdo anything. For her, the Catholic Church stood for religious liberty under law, and that was its appeal. Lest their friendship become too precious to them both, she agreed never again to see the priest who had ushered her into the Church. She worked conscienciously at writing, without in any way neglecting her seven children (the eighth had died). This admirable and at times almost heroic discipline is reflected by her poetry and prose.

But of the wild breaking forth of genius her writing shows no trace. Nothing overwhelms her; she is never mysteriously greater than she guesses. Nor was urbane civilization a loss to her: she preferred it. It was only, judging her by the strictest criterion, a loss to literature. For, reading her work, that is tidy as her London flat and immaculate as her estate "Greatham" in Sussex, one pays well-meant honest compliments—many compliments—while longing for a morass where roots plunder down deep and reckless, and trees rear so high one cannot count the leaves. One longs (which is perhaps an impertinence and certainly a futility) for the minor poet to metamorphose into a major poet. No great battle, it seems, was ever fought on the field of her soul. What was there to fight over?—the elements of her nature were thoroughly in accord and under control. At the news of the death of her good friend Coventry Patmore, she withdrew into a dark room for a while—that was all—and came out, if not serene, quiet. It might be argued that she distilled the essence from passion, and therefore knew what passion was. But the splendid flavour from the mighty grapes is not there; he who drinks is not deceived into thinking the vintage is of the first. Her writing is the zenith of journalism; it is a little better than that. But it is not (to hazard another figure) that she drops a vast net into the sea and is surprised at her own catch. She wants a fish and a fish she catches. Its silver scales glisten and sparkle. But some have dragged the sea and brought up a great whale, thrashing.

Portraits of Alice, who was dark, and of her sister Elizabeth, who was blonde, make it easy to believe that her mother, who had been Christina Weller, the pianist, was considered by her husband, Thomas James Thompson, and their close friend, Charles Dickens, a great beauty. Alice grew to womanhood without losing those same great eyes. Sargent's drawing of her stresses an ethereal look not caused entirely by precarious health, being a quality of soul. Under the high cheek-bones are hollows, the delicate long nose is slightly arched, and the mouth gentle.

Elizabeth, who as Lady Butler became a celebrated painter of war pictures, and Alice, who became perhaps the best-known woman writer of her day, testify to the intelligence of their father, who had taught them as if they were sons. Mrs. Meynell wrote, after his death,

"How should he not have loved all arts, in which his choice was delicate, liberal, instructed, studious, docile, austere?"

And in "A Remembrance,"

"Loving literature, he never lifted a pen except to write a letter. He was not inarticulate, he was only silent. He had an exquisite style from which to refrain."

In "A Father of Women" she cries to him for similarity:

> O liberal, constant, dear!
> Crush in my nature the ungenerous art
> Of the inferior . . .

And, after the World War,

> The crippled world! Come, then,
> Fathers of women with your honour in trust.
> Approve, accept, know them daughters of men,
> Now that your sons are dust.

She was found weeping because once, long ago, her father had asked her to walk with him and she had refused.

The Catholic Church, which her mother, sister and father joined, was a never-relaxing influence on her life. She wrote a priest,

"I received the Church so that whatever She could unfold with time she would unfold there where I had enclosed her, in my heart."

In younger years she practiced mortification, in later years, poetry—both expressions of religious feeling.

> Thou art the way.
> Hadst Thou been nothing but the goal,
>   I cannot say
> If Thou hadst ever met my soul.
>
>   I cannot see—
> I, child of process—if there lies
>   An end for me,
> Full of repose, full of replies.
>
>   I'll not reproach
> The way that goes, my feet that stir.
>   Access, approach,
> Art Thou, time, way and wayfarer.

Marriage, to her, was a sacrament. Wilfred Meynell, also a Catholic convert, had wanted to meet her because he liked a poem quoted in the *Pall Mall Gazette,* "Thy Heart Shall Be My Garden." Their years together were agitated by his editorship of *The Pen, The Weekly Register,* and finally the excellent *Merrie England.* When copy was short, which was frequently, the busy mother became chief anonymous contributor. Her first book of poems, *Preludes,* had been published when she was twenty-five, before her marriage. Now she repudiated it; but many critics earnestly defended "Renouncement," which Dante Gabriel Rossetti knew by heart, and "To a Daisy" (rather reminiscent of Tennyson's "Flower in the Crannied Wall"), and "A Letter from a Girl to Her Own Old Age," the last verse of which, together with the whole of "San Lorenzo," Ruskin called the finest things he had yet seen or felt in modern verse, and "Song of the Night at Daybreak":

> All my stars forsake me,
> And the dawn-winds shake me.
> Where shall I betake me?
>
> Whither shall I run
> Till the set of sun,
> Till the day be done?
>
> To the mountain-mine,
> To the boughs o' the pine,
> To the blind man's eyne.
>
> To a brow that is
> Bowed upon the knees,
> Sick with memories.

When she proposed to revise the book, Francis Thompson wrote her a long letter, ending,

"I conjure Alice Meynell to leave us Alice Thompson, unimproved, unsophisticated, with her weakness and her strength as we saw, accepted, admired and loved her."

She was thirty-nine when she began to send essays to W. E. Henley, editor of *The National Observer*. Four years later they were collected under the title, *The Rhythm of Life,* and published simultaneously with her *Poems.* Coventry Patmore's dictum in the *Fortnightly Review* was typical of the latter's reception:

"This, like all Mrs. Meynell's verse, is true, beautiful, tender, and negatively almost faultless; but it does not attain the classical and only sound standard."

Of the essays he said,

"At least half of this little volume is *classical* work, embodying as it does a new thought of general and permanent significance in perfect language, and bearing, in every sentence, the hall-mark of genius, namely, the marriage of masculine force of insight with feminine grace and tact of expression."

She published other essays and poems: a careful study of Ruskin, an anthology, *The Children of the Old Masters,* selections from Patmore's and Father Tabb's poems, and *Mary, Mother of Jesus.* There are no more delightful essays on children in English than hers in *The Darling Young.* But time has not shifted very much the emphasis of that first judgment.

Nor was Patmore the only famous friend: there were Aubrey Vere, Katherine Tynan, George Meredith, and Francis Thompson (whom she and her husband had rescued and taken care of, when he was almost destroyed by laudanum), to name only a few.

Francis Thompson dedicated to her an exquisite sequence of poems called "Love in Dian's Lap," in which he becomes pure spirit in order to love her honourably, and of which, Patmore said, Beatrice or Laura might have been proud.

> This soul which on your soul is laid,
> As maid's breast against breast of maid.

She requited his impassioned allegiance with the patience his warped and haphazard way of living necessitated.

"Francis Thompson has just arrived," she wrote once, "at about eight-thirty, to the seven o'clock dinner, or rather to the one-thirty luncheon, for that was the meal he chose, as he was going to confession tonight. I think it is the same confession that kept him many moons ago."

His nervous eccentricites increased with time, consumption being aggravated by laudanum poisoning. One day when an umbrella fell against him he said seriously, trembling: "I am the target of all disasters!" But Alice Meynell when she looked at him saw a man of genius.

George Meredith grew, in a special frame, large double white violets for her, a variety which she had loved in Genoa in her childhood. It was he who had called her writing "princely journalism," when she was still an anonymous and unknown contributor to the *Pall Mall Gazette,* and who wrote, later, of her essays,

"The surprise coming on us from their combined grace of manner and sanity of thought is like one's dream of what the recognition of a new truth would be."

After his death she wrote her mother:

"I feel the loss of George Meredith is a very great one. . . .
No one knew him as I did. He told me that I could have
made him what he should have been, and what he could
not be without me. He calculated whether there had been
a time when he was a widower and I unmarried when we
might have met. A retrospective offer!"

Monica, her eldest daughter, who saw how everyone
was enchanted and enchained by her mother's rare
quality, strove, in the following hand-delivered letter,
to be original by being stern:

"Dear Mother,—I hope you will in time give up your absurd
thoughts about literature. It makes my mind get quite feverish when I think of the exhaltation your undergoing. Now
mother take my advice and don't be quite so estatic, you'll
get on just as well in the world and much better because
you'll be respected. Now just you see.

Monnie."

So much was safe, at the end, for one who liked things
ordered and neat—not only her children and grandchildren, but pure words laid away in paragraphs. Did
she remember them during the seven weeks of her last
illness? From "Domus Augusta,"

"But, doubtless, right language enlarges the soul as no other
power or influence may do. . . ."

From "Rain,"

"Not excepting the falling stars—for they are far less sudden—there is nothing in nature that so outstrips our unready eyes as the familiar rain. . . ."

From "The Tethered Constellations," speaking of stars reflected in water,

"On a darker and more vacant field than that of the real skies, the shape of the Lyre or the Bear has an altogether new and noble solitude. . . ."

From "Rushes and Reeds,"

"Taller than the grass and lower than the trees, there is yet another growth that feels the implicit spring. . . ."

From "The Honours of Mortality," a defense of "hack work" well done,

"The honour of the day is for ever the honour of that day. It goes into the treasury of things that are honestly and completely ended and done with. . . ."

From "The Rhythm of Life,"

"If life is not always poetical, it is at least metrical. Periodicity rules over the mental experience of man, according to the path of the orbit of his thoughts. Distances are not gauged, ellipses not measured, velocities not ascertained, times not known. Nevertheless, the recurrence is sure. . . ."

From "The Colour of Life,"

"Red has been praised for its nobility as the colour of life. But the true colour of life is not red. Red is the colour of violence, or of life broken open, edited, and published. . . . The true colour of life is the colour of the body, the colour of the covered red, the implicit and not explicit red of the living heart and the pulses. . . ."

From "The Horizon,"

"To mount a hill is to lift with you something lighter and brighter than yourself or than any meaner burden. You lift the world, you raise the horizon; you give a signal for the distance to stand up. It is like the scene in the Vatican when a Cardinal, with his dramatic Italian hands, bids the kneeling groups to arise. He does more than bid them. He lifts them, he gathers them up, far and near, with the upward gesture of both arms; he takes them to their feet. . . ."

From "Fellow Travelers with a Bird,"

"To attend to a living child is to be baffled in your humour, disappointed of your pathos, and set freshly free from all the preoccupations. You cannot anticipate him. Blackbirds, overheard year by year, do not compose the same phrases; never two leitmotifs alike. Not the tune, but the note alters. So with the uncovenanted ways of a child you keep no tryst. They meet you at another place, after failing you where you tarried. . . ."

From "The Illusion of Historic Time,"

"Childhood is itself Antiquity—to every man his only Antiquity."

And from "The Flower,"

"What, for novelty, what, for singleness, what, for separateness, can equal the last? Of many thousand kisses the poor last—but even the kisses of your mouth are all numbered."

Each part of Alice Meynell's mind and life fitted into the whole, without friction of rust. But one would hardly have predicted that she would say what she did say on her deathbed, at seventy-three—she who had wished to live, as passionately as if young: "This is not tragic. I am happy."

Indeed in old age she almost belied the implication of her life, that she had no suddenness, no secret, no unexpected impulse; almost made perjury of her younger years. During the zeppelin raids in the World War, when the bravest cowered in London cellars shuddering, she was elated. She stared up into the threatening heavens. Her bright eyes shone.

XIII

ELIZABETH BARRETT BROWNING

T HERE are no certainties, science claims—only high degrees of probability. Then we will say that there was a high degree of probability that the Victorian Era would produce an Elizabeth Barrett, since every period strives after its perfect symbol. She was just retiring, and erudite, and effusive enough. She belonged in the Victorian picture, not as archaically as an antimacassar, but as truly. When she married Robert Browning, who had already published *Paracelsus, Sordello, Blot on the 'Scutcheon* and *Bells and Pomegranates,* it is said that a London newspaper, after much loud vaunting of the "bride who is a famous poetess," added, "Mr. Browning also writes."

But nineteenth century praise carried a penalty, all unsuspected: twentieth century scorn. Today few read the verse-novel, *Aurora Leigh,* which the author called "the most mature of my works," except dry souls, who complain that her didacticism is dry. Graduate students in seminar courses, when assigned her *Poetical Works,* skip the translations from Homer, Theocritus, Apuleius, Nonnus, Hesiod, Aeschylus, Euripides, Bion and Anacreon, to pause wistfully but not long at "To Flush, My Dog," which is mildly interesting as biography, and "The Deserted Garden" and "Cowper's Grave," which have the virtue of simplicity though not brevity, and "Casa Guidi Windows," a prosy but sincere tribute to Italy. There is no getting around the fact that Elizabeth Barrett Browning, for all her great romantic reputation, means very little to the sensitive modern mind. On the wall of Casa Guidi in Florence the Italians have carved this inscription:

"Qui scrisse e morì Elizabetta Barrett Browning, che in cuore di donna conciliava scienza di dotto e spirito di poeta, e fece del suo verso aureo annello fra Italia e Inghilterra. Pone questa lapide Firenze grata 1861."

In the heart of the new generation is no similar inscription. Grateful for what? they say. Sentimentality?

But the twentieth century must beware lest, in relieving one side of an overburdened scale, it throw the weight violently to the other and disturb that undeviating balance which is truth; must beware lest, in its zeal for criticizing false exuberances, it forget "Consolation" and "Grief" and certain lines from the *Sonnets from the Portuguese.* This Victorian lady with almost owlishly large eyes, and an impressively spacious brow, wore a flock of dark curls on either side of her face, which a modern woman would push back impatiently; but they became her very well.

To consider Elizabeth Barrett dispassionately it is necessary to separate her for a while, rather sternly, from Robert Browning. All the world loves a lover; but Elizabeth Barrett lived almost forty years without Browning before she lived fifteen years with him.

Born in 1806, at Coxhoe Hall, Durham, England,

she was the eldest child of Edward Barrett Moulton, who took Barrett as a surname on succeeding to his maternal grandfather's rich estates in Jamaica. She lost her mother while still young, and grew ever closer to her father—a cold, passionate man who later, on principle, was to forbid his daughters to marry. No one, he thought, was good enough for them. He wanted them home.

At ten his pupil and favourite daughter Elizabeth read Homer in the original; at eleven composed "a great epic in four books," *The Battle of Marathon,* of which her father printed fifty copies; at nineteen published an *Essay on Mind;* at thirty-two *The Seraphim;* and at thirty-eight *Poems,* in which she paid a graceful tribute to Robert Browning, whom she had not met, but from whom came, she well knew, an occasional

"Pomegranate, which if cut deep down the middle,
Shows a heart within blood-tinctured, of a veined humanity."

But famed for sagacity from childhood up, with a doting family and many laudatory friends—Miss Mitford, R. H. Horne, John Kenyon, Walter Savage Landor—with a silk-eared cocker spaniel named Flush, and with a comfortable, even handsome home, first in sight of the beautiful Malvern Hills, then in green Devon, and finally on a dignified street in London—the lady had the perversity not to be happy.

In early childhood she had had a spinal affection,

and her lungs had become delicate, and when the
Barretts moved to London a blood vessel had broken
and, as an invalid, she had been sent for three years to
Torquay, in the South, for the sun. There in Babba-
combe Bay Edward, her favourite brother among eight,
had been drowned, after she had parted from him that
day, as she said, "with pettish words." The memory of
Edward's drowning made a darkness all around her.
She worked hard at her poetry, as she lay on her habitual
sofa, in the house at 50 Wimpole Street, trying to dispel
the cloud. It was generally understood in the household that dear Elizabeth would not live long. But when
her doctor said that English winters were slowly
weakening her, and that her one chance of recovery was
Italy, Mr. Barrett snapped that it was never to be
mentioned again.

Then one day she wrote a friend,

"I had a letter from Browning the poet which threw me into
ecstasies—Browning, the author of *Paracelsus,* the king of
the mystics."

A correspondence developed between the two poets,
which led after several months to a meeting, and mutual
recognition.

> First time he kissed me, he but only kissed
> The fingers of this hand wherewith I write;
> And ever since, it grew more clean and white,
> Slow to world-greetings, quick with its "Oh list!"
> When the angels speak. A ring of amethyst

I could not wear here plainer to my sight
Than that first kiss. The second passed in height
The first, and sought the forehead, and half missed,
Half falling on the hair. Oh beyond meed!
That was the chrism of love, which love's own crown
With sanctifying sweetness did precede.
The third upon my lips was folded down
In perfect purple state; since when, indeed,
I have been proud and said, "My love, my own."

She was six years older than he; and supposedly possessed of an incurable ailment and doomed to pass the rest of her life on a couch; her father would never consent to a marriage—but she was in love just the same. She hesitated, having a regard for his liberty, and refused him "with all my will, but much against my heart"; and then accepted him in the end because his passionate insistence made their union inevitable. Browning was reluctant to deceive her father. She alone knew how imperative was deception.

They were married secretly, in September, 1846, in Marylebone Parish Church, with no one from 50 Wimpole Street to witness or bless, except her maid Wilson. Her two sisters, who knew of her engagement, had not been told of the marriage plan, lest their father's wrath crush them as it fell. For a week Mrs. Browning remained in her father's house. Then with Flush and Wilson and a devoted and inexhaustable husband, she crossed to the Continent.

The story of Mr. Barrett's opposition is not an attempt to make an ogre out of him. He has been contorted out of human shape by writers who find it easy and tempting to juxtapose Mr. Browning as hero with Mr. Barrett as villain. But there is no doubt that Elizabeth loved and feared and, in time, resented him exceedingly, and that the tearing of his shadow from her life was, to her, painful and momentous. Only two years before her flight, in dedicating her poems to him, she had wished to

"conjure your beloved image between myself and the public . . . and satisfy my heart, while I sanctify my ambition, by associating with the great pursuit of my life its tenderest and holiest affection."

However wrong and tyrannical she came to believe him, however compensating her new relation with Browning was, she must have suffered under her father's refusal to forgive her, to the day of her death.

Because the climate was good and living not expensive, the two poets settled in Florence, temporarily on the blue hills of Fiesole, and permanently in a substantial if modest old palace, Casa Guidi, across from San Felice Church and around the corner from the immense grey Pitti. Casa Guidi is of stone, with many rooms of cavernous ceiling and a balcony of "lozenge brick-work sprinkled cool." Once in a while they took a trip to Rome, or Siena, or Pisa, and twice to England; but they loved and identified themselves with Florence. After fifteen years of well-nigh flawless happiness, Mrs.

Browning, with touching appropriateness, died there in her husband's arms. She had produced many poems, and a son named Robert Weidemann Barrett Browning, who was to become a sculptor, and at last she could rest. Her husband buried her in the Protestant cemetery in Florence, that green island of the dead, beautiful with cypresses, and reared over her a tomb designed on classical lines, within sight through tangled roses of the grave of Walter Savage Landor; and with his heart full, fled away to London, to Paris, to Venice, never to return to lovely and beneficent Florence, to be mocked at by memories. Forever, now, he wanted to avoid the time-encrusted streets, where so much that was heroic had happened to Italy, and so much that was idyllic had happened to him and to her; wanted to avoid lordly San Miniato which they had walked up to together; and Santa Maria Novella where they had looked into the eyes of God, in Massacio's great picture, and knelt side by side; and the Loggia where Elizabeth had admired Cellini's "Perseus" and the antique Menelaus with the body of Patroclus; and the Porta Romana, in the gloom of which they had strolled of an evening, with Flush running ahead, smelling the ground; and the Ponte Vecchio loaded with jewelry shops; and the silver-coiled Arno; and the Tuscan hills grey with olives, in the peculiarly transparent and delicate Tuscan air. . . . The quality of a particular happiness, when it is gone, is gone. "O lyric love," he cried,

> half angel and half bird
> And all a wonder and a wild desire,—
> Boldest of hearts that ever braved the sun . . .
> And sang a kindred soul out to his face . . .

Is utter happiness the atmosphere in which art flowers? The lives of the Brownings will not answer the question. He wrote less poetry during his marriage than before or after; but she seems to have written as much poetry during her marriage as before, and some was good, and some poor, as before. But in one respect at least the years in Florence helped her writing: she learned to be less the orator and savant; less complicated in her emotions; probably because her life, which had been so long cramped inward, was drawn outward by family affection, under the warm Italian sun. Indeed her interest expanded beyond her family and became ardently involved in the Italian struggle for unity, which was to be achieved through Garibaldi and Cavour and which she foresaw in "Casa Guidi Windows":

> I heard last night a little child go singing
>   'Neath Casa Guidi windows, by the church,
> *"O bella libertà, O bella! . . ."*

It seemed but right and fitting that throughout the length and breadth of Italy there should be solidarity and freedom, as under the daintily scrolled ceiling at Casa Guidi.

But though love fulfilled Elizabeth Barrett, love cannot be said to have directly inspired her highest poetry. Browning exclaimed, after being shown in Pisa (or was

184

it Bagni di Lucca?) the so-called *Sonnets from the Portuguese* which she had written for him in secret and with no thought of publication: "I dared not reserve to myself the finest sonnets written in any language since Shakespeare's"; but surely he was biassed by love, for only seven or eight of the forty-four are, strictly appraised, first class; though strongly dramatic by reason of a large emotion, they are in continual danger of becoming sentimental.

> Straight way I was 'ware,
> So weeping, how a mystic shape did move
> Behind me, and drew me backward by the hair;
> And a voice said in mastery, while I strove,
> "Guess now who holds thee?"—"Death," I said.
>   But there
> The silver answer rang, "Not Death, but Love."

And,

> Unlike are we, unlike, O Princely Heart!
> Unlike our uses and our destinies.
> Our ministering two angels look surprise
> On one another as they strike athwart
> Their wings in passing. . . .

And the famous one which begins,

> If thou must love me, let it be for naught
> Except for love's sake only. . . .

And,

> How do I love thee? Let me count the ways.
> I love thee to the depth and breadth and height
> My soul can reach, when feeling out of sight

185

For the ends of being and ideal grace.
I love thee to the level of every day's
Most quiet need, by sun and candlelight.
I love thee freely, as men strive for right.
I love thee purely, as they turn from praise. . . .

And, perhaps the noblest:

When our two souls stand up erect and strong,
Face to face, silent, drawing nigh and nigher,
Until the lengthening wings break into fire
At either curved point, what bitter wrong
Can the earth do to us, that we should not long
Be here contented? Think. In mounting higher,
The angels would press on us, and aspire
To drop some golden orb of perfect song
Into our deep, dear silence. Let us stay
Rather on earth, beloved, where the unfit
Contrarious moods of men recoil away,
And isolate pure spirits, and permit
A place to stand and love in for a day,
With darkness and the death-hour rounding it.

These expressions of love have power to move, but, except infrequently, they are too much an attitude. They are too agitated; too, one might almost say, abundant; they become, at times, hysterical, representing what Mrs. Browning thought love should be, rather than what it is. They are overbright like the eyes of a fever patient, with accelerated pulse. Her intellect simply does not keep pace with her emotions. The flesh, of the poem, so to speak, is without a sufficient bony structure underneath it, to support and give it tone. For a hint of the impassioned quiet which the great, who are sure of themselves, have felt, one must read one of her poems not on the subject of love at all— "Grief":

> I tell you hopeless grief is passionless;
> That only men incredulous of despair,
> Half-taught in anguish, through the midnight air
> Beat upward to God's throne in loud access
> Of shrieking and reproach. Full desertness,
> In souls as countries, lieth silent-bare
> Under the blanching, vertical eye-glare
> Of the absolute heavens. Deep-hearted man, express
> Grief for thy dead in silence like to death—
> Most like a monumental statue set
> In everlasting watch and moveless woe
> Till itself crumble in the dust beneath.
> Touch it; the marble eyelids are not wet:
> If it could weep, it could arise and go.

An artist has the right to be judged by her best work.

XIV

CHARLOTTE MEW

Nοτ many years ago there lived in Bloomsbury a tiny woman who had a small squarish hand like a sensitive man's, rather square shoulders, a thin mouth in which was no cruelty, hair thick and alive which "disgusted her by turning white," and clear dark blue eyes which startled by being startled; and she chose to wear a man's overcoat; and though poor and hindered kept a rapt obstinate faith in a devious but existent good; and her father a distinguished architect had died early, and her adored mother died late, and then her sister Anne whom ·she loved inordinately died in agony, and when the pressure was too great on her heart, sick and lonely, she died in a London nursing home by drinking lysol; and this woman, though few realized it, then or afterwards, had greatness in her.

Greatness? That is a dangerous word, to be used charily. If it is bandied about loosely and ignorantly, the dead are wronged. Since the beginning of the world there have lived only a few poets of first rank, and almost no women: Sappho; perhaps Emily Brontë; at her best Christina Rossetti; some of the time Emily Dickinson; and apparently, in a flash at the end, Elinor Wylie. The rest had sediment; they were not clear; a cloud floated in the depth of each stream, and so they died, and were buried, and deserve to be forgotten.

Charlotte Mew (1869-1928) was not quite great, but she had greatness in her, not in quantity, for she left only two small volumes, one posthumous, but in crystal and indubitable quality. The work is uneven. If she were alive she would no doubt destroy many published poems, and wise critics would applaud. Certainly the *Early Poems,* which foreshadow the later, should have been allowed to moulder in *The Yellow Book, The English-woman, The Nation, The New Statesman,* and *The Chapbook,* in which, with some of her odd essays and stories, they first appeared. The all but perfect remainder would insure the immortality she was too humble to expect.

It is difficult to sketch a life in which very little happened, and that little was largely concealed. One states, boldly, the bounding dates—whereupon a grey fog of myth, of conjecture, begins to rise and to deceive by exaggerating and diminishing shapes.

A handful of friends testify to her wit, and charm, and incorruption, and to her love of truth for its own sake, which was the underpinning and solid foundation of her being. If she disliked anyone she shut her mouth tightly. She liked to play all sorts of practical jokes. She would be angry suddenly and, as suddenly, calm. According to one friend, she knew how to swear lustily, but was harmless and generous and kind. One day she flung down at the piano, crying, "Now see what that chaste old gentleman will feel"—

and played Bach as he had never been played before. And one day when asked to read her own poetry, she walked back and forth furiously, refusing a chair, throwing down cigarette after cigarette, and then began to recite abruptly—says a friend, Mrs. Dawson-Scott—"in a raucous Cockney voice, but somehow just right, with the right vibration."

In 1923, when the peculiar woman was fifty-four, Thomas Hardy, John Masefield and Walter de la Mare saw to it that she was given a Civil List pension of seventy-five pounds a year. But the rain came too late in the drouth. After the death of the two she loved most, her ground was parched: nothing would grow. Starvation is not the only scourge; it is not the body alone which thirsts and must be quenched. She tried a while longer, without hope, and then decided not to try.

Is this all? Is there no record of the gayety in Paris, or the slow formation of passionate belief, or the love which taught her by frustration and tortured from despair exquisite love poems? Almost nothing —because she willed it so. Loneliness demands more loneliness: there is no breaking the painful and loved habit. She was like the maid in her "The Farmer's Bride" who "wasn't a woman—more like a little frightened fay," and we have to run after her, seize her, and fetch her home.

But how? Only by reading the poems. They are

the fruit of a life, and in them, implicit, are the leaves and branches, the roots and the sap of that tree. What the poems are must be sensed; it is not a matter of logic: only the purest feeling can intercept and interpret. And autobiography should not be charged too often lest the picture be falsified and the soul denied its privilege of vicarious experience. Who, without misgivings, could assert that Charlotte Mew is the Farmer's Bride who fears all men as such, or the reproacher of another Judas in that searing poem, "Friend, Wherefore—?" or the tragic "Madeleine in Church" who has it out with God? Yet there are resemblances, and one hears in the voice that extra and convincing quality which is personal and inevitable anguish, not anguish assumed.

At least thirty poems out of some sixty in *The Farmer's Bride* and *The Rambling Sailor* (not counting the *Early Poems*) are beyond all description limpid and fine. They are intelligent but not intellectual; and though emotional, not heavily so. By the lightest means, the most wistful, the most poignant, the most circling and purposeless and yet the most sure, they break the heart. The short ones like "Sea Love," evanescent finality, and *"Fin de Fête,"* mighty indirection, which Thomas Hardy kept among his papers, would be ruined by one off note; but the pitch is absolutely true. The long poems pile impression on impression, image on image, perhaps factually but never emotionally unrelated, so that they carry the greatest possible burden of meaning. Strange and opposite things are juxtaposed in a way which should sound jerky, in long lines which by all the rules should be unwieldy, and the effect is wonderful, is devastating. Compression was impossible: their essential meaning, like that of a life, is not single, but a subtle mingling of diverse elements. The separate ideas usually begin and end on the same line, they do not run over; yet the lines are extraordinarily flexible. When May Sinclair criticized her friend's "apparent lack of metrical technique," Miss Mew answered coolly, "Of course I could write smoothly if I chose."

It is as if, in her poetry, she were always protesting against the inert and lifeless, the alien thing which beckons us and rejects us. In "Fame" she turns

> Back to the old known things that are the new,
> The folded glory of the gorse, the sweet-briar air,
> To the larks that cannot praise us, knowing nothing
> of what we do . . .

In "Nunhead Cemetery" she watches the digging and the decorating of graves, and experiences a bitter throe.

> There is something horrible about a flower;
> This, broken in my hand, is one of those
> He threw in just now: it will not live another hour;
> There are thousands more: you do not miss a rose.

"Beside the Bed" and "To a Child in Death" are the more beautiful because they cannot be analyzed. Here is a desperation made gentle and still:

Because all night you have not turned to us or spoken,
    It is time for you to wake; your dreams were never very
        deep:
I, for one, have seen the thin, bright, twisted threads of them
        dimmed suddenly and broken,
    This is only a most piteous pretense of sleep.

It was not only the children who, to her, were trying to gather pieces of shadow:

    "I've got one," cried sister to brother.
      "I've got two." "Now I've got another."
    But scudding away on their little feet
      They left the shade in the sunny street.

"Old Shepherd's Prayer" divines the heart of a simple old man about to die, who prays,

Heavenly Master, I wud like to wake to they same green
    places
Where I be know'd for breakin' dogs and follerin' sheep.
And if I may not walk in th' old ways and look on th'
    old faces
I wud sooner sleep.

In her musing she remembers

        rooms that have had their part
    In the steady slowing down of the heart,
    The room in Paris, the room at Geneva,

The little damp room with the seaweed smell,
And that ceaseless maddening sound of the tide—
Rooms where for good or for ill—things died.

And she says, with the wounding simplicity of children,

I so liked Spring last year
  Because you were here;—
Because it was these you so liked to hear—
  I so liked you.

This year's a different thing,—
  I'll not think of you.
But I'll like Spring because it is simply Spring
  As the thrushes do.

And,

Love, Love, today, my dear,
  Love is not always here;
Wise maids know how soon grows sere
The greenest leaf of Spring;
  But no man knoweth
  Whither it goeth
  When the wind bloweth
    So frail a thing.

Love, Love, my dear, today
  If the ship's in the bay,
If the bird has come your way
That sings on summer trees;
  When his song faileth
  And the ship saileth
  No voice availeth
    To call back these.

And, in "Sea Love,"

> Tide be runnin' the great world over:
> 'Twas only last June month I mind that we
> Was thinkin' the toss and the call in the breast of
>   the lover
> So everlastin' as the sea.
>
> Here's the same little fishes that sputter and swim,
> Wi' the moon's old glim on the gray, wet sand;
> An' him no more to me nor me to him
> Than the wind goin' over my hand.

Then the note becomes graver and the volume swells. "I Have Been Through the Gates" is as solemn as Milton, but less pretentious. The "Go through, go through the gates" of Isaiah is answered in lofty mournfulness:

His heart, to me, was a place of palaces and pinnacles and
       shining towers;
I saw it then as we see things in dreams,—I do not remem-
       ber how long I slept;
I remember the trees, and the high, white walls, and how
       the sun was always on the towers;
The walls are standing today, and the gates: I have been
       through the gates, I have groped, I have crept
Back, back. There is dust in the streets and blood; they are
       empty; darkness is over them;
His heart is a place with the lights gone out, forsaken by
       great winds and the heavenly rain, unclean and
       unswept,
Like the heart of the holy city, old, blind, beautiful Jeru-
       salem,
              Over which Christ wept.

But it is the long "Madeleine in Church" which, by varying line and tempo, involves us the most deeply in her human questioning; for it is like the impetuous talk of someone with a heart too full to let the words come out slowly, with precision. I quote only a part of it:

Oh! quiet Christ who never knew
The poisonous fangs that bite us through
   And make us do the things we do,
See how we suffer and fight and die,
   How helpless and how low we lie,
God holds You, and You hang so high,
Though no one looking long at You,
   Can think You do not suffer too,
But, up there, from Your still star-lighted tree
   What can You know, what can You really see
      Of this dark ditch, the soul of me!

We are what we are: when I was half a child I could not sit
Watching black shadows on green lawns and red carnations
      burning in the sun,
   Without paying so heavily for it
That joy and pain, like any mother and her unborn child
      were almost one.
   I could hardly bear
The dreams upon the eyes of white geraniums in the dusk,
   The thick, close voice of musk,
   The jessamine music on the thin night air,
Or sometimes my own hands about me anywhere—
     · · · · · · ·

                No, one cannot see
How it shall be made up to them in some serene eternity.

If there were fifty heavens God could not give us back the
    child who went or never came;
  Here, on our little patch of this great earth, the sun of
    any darkened day,
  Not one of all the starry buds hung on the hawthorne
    trees of last year's May,
    No shadow from the sloping fields of yesterday;
  For every hour they slant across the hedge a different way,
    The shadows are never the same . . .

Shadows were everywhere, but in the country they
hid reality less, she found, than in the congested city;
so she who was city-bred loved the country.

Lord, when I look at lovely things which pass,
  Under old trees the shadows of young leaves
Dancing to please the wind along the grass,
  Or the gold stillness of the August sun on the August
    sheaves;
Can I believe there is a heavenlier world than this?
  And if there is
Will the strange heart of any everlasting thing
  Bring me these dreams that take my breath away?
They come at evening with the home-flying rooks and the
    scent of hay,
  Over the fields. They come in Spring.

In "Moorland Night," with "face hid against the
grass," after much seeking "the Thing is found"; but
she knows "it is not for long in any life." In "The
Trees Are Down" she cannot listen to the sound of
the great plane-trees being cut at the end of the

garden, nor think of what she has loved as dying. Other friends failed her but the creatures of wood and meadow were constant and faithful.

> And from the trees about the farm, not very high,
> A flight of pigeons fluttered up into an early evening
> mackerel sky . . .

Her life spanned from Queen Victoria's reign, across the Great War, into the harsh post-war period, and a continual readjustment was required of a heart peculiarly vulnerable to change. But she was brave, and during the winter of the war could say,

> "Let us remember that Spring will come again . . ."

Once she quoted, "We are all stricken men," but the letter which contained the hollow words was zestful, gallant, and joking.

Then what of the end? We know so little; nothing intimate in the way of facts; only that she went to a nursing home for a not very serious operation and while there took her life.

> Smile, Death, as you fasten the blades to my feet for me,
> On, on let us skate past the sleeping willows dusted with
> snow;
> Fast, fast down the frozen stream, with the moor and the
> road and the vision behind,
> (Show me your face, why the eyes are kind!)
> And we will not speak of life or believe in it or remember
> it as we go.

These are lovely words: not passion but the distillation of passion. Faithful words; for she believed to the finish of the "whole, gay, unbearable, amazing show" that "nothing is true that is not good." And these words, with all the other words in her two thin volumes, are they not (since "in each life there is a spiritual line, an upward curve, and all that adheres to and strengthens this line is our real life—the rest but chaff falling from us as our souls progress") enough of a biography?

XV

GEORGE ELIOT

GEORGE ELIOT (christened Mary Ann Evans) strove all her life to tell people what they should be and do. But she stands today, in many respects, a monumental and all but terrifying example of what a novelist should not be and do. As a novelist she was too often an essayist, a professor of psychology, ethics and history, a Methodist preacher tainted with Positivism. To contemplate her, even in a brief paper, is to be weighed down, like the old man of the sea, with a tragic sense of existence.

Born in 1819 in Warwickshire Mary Ann Evans, with her sister Chrissie and brother Isaac, spent a happy early-childhood at Griff, a "charming red-brick ivy-covered house" with a farmyard surrounding it, on the estate of Francis Newdigate, whose agent her father was. Twice a day the stagecoach rattled up to the gates, and the children rushed out to stare in ecstasy at the postillions and the queer travellers within the dark recess. Mary Ann was the most curious, as she was the most clever, and the most pious, and the most clumsy, and ugly. Clean little Chrissie, who lived in fear of dirtying her pinafore, and her good and energetic though rather formidable mother, she loved; but Isey and her father she followed about like a little dog, adoring, and tried to become more like them by cutting her long hair. But she shuddered in true girl-fashion at baiting Isey's crooked pins with worms, lest she hurt them; and when sent off to boarding school, was afraid to be left in a dark room at night; and after being summoned to the parlour to play the piano for the edification of guests, would fly up to her bedroom and throw herself on the floor in a paroxysm of weeping. Perhaps the excessive self-consciousness of her adolescence was partly the fault of her mirror which showed her, every time she combed her hair, or washed, a face shaped a little like a horse's, with yellowish skin and short-sighted green-blue eyes and hair the colour of dust. As if in an effort to make herself still less presentable, at school she wore for a time, as a sign of her new Calvinistic views, an "anti-supernatural cap." When she was seventeen her mother died, and she left school and settled down to managing the farm and Father: "standing sentinel" over damson cheese by the hour, churning butter, boiling jellies till her hands were unsteady for sewing, running a poultry yard, keeping her father's accounts with meticulous patience, and doing the housework as tidily and intelligently as she had conducted her school-studies. Years later she could say, "I think after all I like a clean kitchen better than any other room." As if not sufficiently burdened, she gave hours to the poor and the sick, and had a master come regularly from Coventry to teach her German and Italian, and another, music, and persevered till she had taught herself Greek and Latin. She read prodigiously, mostly on religious subjects: Wilberforce, Montaigne, and Keble. Pascal's *Pensées* was on the table beside her bed. "And so the poor child," she was to write of Maggie Tulliver, a close approximation of herself,

"with her soul's hunger and her illusions of self-flattery, began to nibble at this thick-rinded fruit of the tree of knowledge . . ."

When she and Isey made a trip to London, her deepest impressions were of Greenwich Hospital and of the great bell of St. Paul's Cathedral, and she refused to go to the theatre with him, saying she preferred to stay in her hotel room, alone, reading the Bible. Already her ideas were crystallizing. She who had stared so long at the level and precise fields of Warwickshire, in endless and inevitable succession, believed that every least act has its inevitable consequence; that we are controlled, from without, by heredity, environment, social traditions and universal laws; and that it is our duty to submit: a cold principle for a young girl. To a devout aunt she bemoaned her "besetments" and "altogether benumbed soul." Her first printed piece of writing, in the *Christian Observer,* when she was twenty, was a metrical farewell to the world. In the library at Arbury Hall, where Mr. Newdigate allowed her to read, she seems not to have missed the pleasant diversions of youth;

and in Coventry, where she and her father lived after her newly married brother took over Griff House and the agency, she went around in unbecoming, even freakish, clothes, as if to announce defiantly that she did not care what anybody thought. It was impossible to imagine her as ever having been less old and staid than she now appeared.

But in Coventry she made friends rather quickly: Charles Bray, a ribbon manufacturer absorbed in the study of phrenology, who had written *The Education of the Feelings* and *The Philosophy of Necessity;* his wife, who had been Caroline Hennell; Caroline's brother Charles, who had written *An Enquiry concerning the Origin of Christianity;* and Caroline's sister Sarah, a stanch deist, who wrote in three volumes *Present Religion as a Faith Owning Friendship with Thought.* In their charming if sometimes ponderous company at Rosehill, the Brays' home, her faith in the Established Church, to which she belonged, and in the Baptist Church, to which she had been exposed, first weakened and then gave way completely. Eleven days after meeting her new friends she wrote Miss Lewis, who had been a beloved schoolteacher:

"My whole soul has been engrossed in the most interesting of all enquiries for the last few days, and to what result my thoughts may lead, I know not, possibly to one that will startle you: but my only desire is to know the truth, my only fear to cling to error."

Soon she was refusing to accompany her father to
Matins, and the good man was calling it a monstros-
ity and putting his house into the hands of agents so
that he could go and live with Chrissie. She stood her
ground. But the Brays suggested that social relations
were based on mutual concessions, and chided her for
making her old father miserable, and at last Mary
Ann (or Marian, as she now preferred to be called)
consented to re-enter the suspect portals. Her life
was now intensely interesting. With her free-think-
ing friends she went on delightful excursions to
Wales, Scotland, the Lake Country, Stratford and
Malvern. Under their influence she undertook to
translate Strauss' *Leben Jesu*: "leathery Strauss,"
she called it, but laboured at it three years, for the
privilege of anonymity and the magnificent sum of
twenty pounds. Then she began, in a fever, to translate Spinoza's *Tractatus Theologico-Politicus*. But
the life she had been building up was unexpectedly
shattered, for her father died one bleak day, and she
found herself thirty and alone, with the meagerest
of annuities, and could not but cry,

"What shall I do without my father? It will seem as if a
part of my moral nature were gone."

Her new life of independence was inaugurated by
a trip to the Continent with the Brays, where she
stayed for eight months, first in a *pension* in Geneva,

and then in lodgings at the home of Madame D'Albert Durade, whose husband was a painter; and was confirmed by sixteen tranquil months as a guest of the Brays at Rosehill. There she wrote her first real article: a review of Mackay's *Progress of the Intellect,* which was published unsigned (as were all reviews at that time) in the *Westminster Review,* an organ for free-thinkers edited by John Chapman, a good editor but notorious philanderer. In London, to which she migrated, she lived at Mr. Chapman's fantastic boarding-house in the Strand, to the discomfort of Mrs. Chapman, who was jealous, with how much or how little cause we do not know.

Here began the struggle between her intellect and heart, between her iron sense of duty and her natural inclinations, which was to mean the disruption of her life, and the healing of it. Or perhaps it had begun earlier, when at twenty-four she is supposed to have met at the home of her half-sister Fanny a young artist, and become engaged to him, and then, virtuously, when her father disapproved, broken with him. In any case her position in the office of the *Westminster* where now, as assistant editor, she was writing most of the reviews as well as proof-reading, threw her among the most brilliant authors of her day—Carlyle, Froude, Harriet Martineau, John Stuart Mill, Francis Newman—and it is not surprising that her life-long yearning for affection and her disposition to lean on some man should have brought her swiftly to a confused issue. Herbert Spencer, the philosopher, who had as much comeliness as brain, was her companion at the theatre and the opera; and for long evenings in Chapman's garden which ran all the way down to the Thames, and to which he loaned them a key, they talked of human happiness and the categoric imperative. "The greatness of her intellect conjoined with her womanly qualities and manner," he admitted, "generally keep me by her side. . . ." And Marian said that

"my brightest spot, next to my love of old friends, is the delicious calm new friendship that Herbert Spencer gives me."

But he was not to be her love; he did not propose, and she does not appear to have been broken-hearted: that troubled privilege was reserved for George Henry Lewes, "a sort of miniature Mirabeau" whom Herbert Spencer introduced to her in a shop, and then brought to call on her at Chapman's bohemian boarding-house.

Her "marriage" to this George Henry Lewes, without benefit of clergy since his flighty run-away wife could not be divorced, was a fair covenant, for twenty-five years honestly kept by them both. He had been a preacher and a medical student, and was now a successful author; his ugliness matched hers, as if expressly made to comfort her; and his temperament, which was protective, admirably supplemented hers, which was clinging. To carry on and conceal their liaison, which she had convinced herself was justified under the circumstances, she moved from the Chapmans' house to private lodgings in Hyde Park Square; and in her contentment wrote on her thirty-fourth birthday:

"I begin this year more happily than I have done most years of my life. We may both find ourselves at the end of the year going faster to the hell of conscious moral and intellectual weakness, still there is a possibility, even a probability, the other way."

But when Lewes fell ill, threatened with softening of the brain, she decided that, since they had become absolutely necessary to each other, and this pillar-and-post life could not continue, she had no choice but to unite herself with him openly, for better or for worse. She and Lewes set off for Antwerp, Weimar and Berlin, where he was looking up material for his *Life of Goethe;* and when, eight months later, they returned to England unrepentant, the die was cast. Her family disowned her; the liberal-minded Brays started out by being silent and frowning: only a few friends would see her at all. But ostracism had its great advantage: with five people to support—the legal Mrs. Lewes and her three children (only one of whom was by Lewes), and Lewes' mother—they could work without the slightest interruption.

Marian's scathing essays for the *Leader* and the *Westminster* were laboured; they rambled, instead of proceeding from one clear point to another; and Lewes began to urge her to write fiction. One morning in a dreamy frame of mind she imagined herself writing a story called *The Sad Fortunes of the Reverend Amos Barton,* and the always-admiring Lewes leaped up and exclaimed in delight: "What a capital title!"

Thus was freed, in a woman's late thirties, a prodigious literary talent, which was to produce *Scenes of Clerical Life,* a group of stories, and then in fairly rapid succession the novels *Adam Bede, The Mill on the Floss* and *Silas Marner,* charming and faithful reconstructions of her Warwickshire days, *Romola,* a less convincing reconstruction of fifteenth-century Florence, which expounds her creed of retribution, *Felix Holt, the Radical,* a poor platform of her political ideas, *Middlemarch,* a magnificent and almost epic return to Warwickshire, and *Daniel Deronda,* a defense of Judaism; as well as many translations, notably Strauss' *Essence of Christianity* and Spinoza's *Ethics,* and some heavy poetry, *The Spanish Gypsy* and *The Legend of Jubal,* and a book of leaden essays, *The Opinions of Theophrastus Such.*

From a delightful writer, with some humour and a gift for remembering the homely details of country life, she who used the pen name George Eliot shrivelled into a stern moral philosopher, "going doggedly to work, seeing what determination can do in the face of despair." As soon as she left the scenes she knew from intimate association, her plots became wooden and her characters types instead of individuals. After *Adam Bede,* writing was never a joy to her. She said that in collecting historical data about Savonarola and his times, *Romola* made her an old woman. Lewes asked her once why her novels were so sad, and with tears in her eyes she answered that she could not help it, life was sad. One of her poems begins, incredibly, "I have a friend, a vegetarian seer, by name Elias Baptist Butterworth." If only Lewes could have warned her. But Lewes never told her anything unfavourable but carefully censored her newspapers by clipping out any adverse allusions. They might make his dear "Polly" feel bad.

If she took herself very seriously, so did her contemporaries. It is related that, after she and Lewes had returned from one of their many trips to the Continent, and Lewes had been made editor of the *Fortnightly Review,* they gave solemn Sunday-evenings at which George Eliot, a little frumpish, a little gauche, famous and in black silk, presided like a pontiff, permitting questions and intoning answers in a vast ritual. One of her admirers compiled an anthology of these "wise, witty and tender" ecclesiastical bulls.

What had happened to the girl who had

"adjusted the broad leaves that set off the pale, fragrant butter as the primrose is set off by its nest of green,"

and had understood and loved the unpretentiousness of Adam Bede who

"knew a fine sight more o' the natur o' things than those as thought themselves his betters,"

and praised the soundness of the inimitable Mrs. Poyser whose wisdom rolled so naturally from her tongue:

"Ah, it's all very fine having a ready-made rich man, but may-happen he'll be a ready-made fool; and it's no use filling your pocket full of money if you've got a hole in the corner. It'll do you no good to sit in a spring cart o' your own, if you've got a soft to drive you: he'll soon turn you over into the ditch. I allays say I'd never marry a man as had got no brains; for where's the use of a woman having brains of her own if she's tackled to a geck as everybody's a-laughing at? She might as well dress herself fine to sit back'ards on a donkey."

In time, around correct Victorian tea-tables, people began to urge "extenuating circumstances"; the best families received her—though they did not introduce her to their unmarried daughters. But she herself always felt morally on the defensive against a public which acclaimed her the equal of Dickens and Thackeray and Scott, and the superior of Trollope, Bulwer Lytton and Charlotte Brontë. The tenets of her evangelical upbringing could not be cancelled from her being. "Her life was governed by a faith she no longer possessed." Having a sense of guilt, she punished her heroines inexorably: Hetty Sorel for sinning, and a part of her sin was her beauty; Maggie Tulliver for going against her family for the sake of a man; Gwendoline Harleth for longing to be rich. With the single-mindedness of a Greek fury, she was avenging what seemed to her subconscious, transgressions. Thus literature became in her hands, not forgiveness, but accusation, and a system of plaguing. Yeats says that

"George Eliot had a fierceness hardly to be found but in a woman turned argumentive, but the habit of mind her fierceness gave its life to was characteristic of her century. . . . She grew up in a century of utilitarianism, when nothing about a man seemed important except his utility to the State, and nothing so useful to the State as the actions whose effect can be weighed by reason."

A strange woman, strong, yet timid. We search the portrait painted by Monsieur D'Albert Durade in Rome, for corroboration of this conflict of interests, or a denial of it. A strange face: one's glance travels a long way from her mouth to her eye; the features are solid and substantial, like age-old rocks set in the earth: they promise a ponderous right judgment, but the expression shows little confidence in the judgment when made.

"Everything in her aspect and presence," said a contemporary Victorian, who had joined the pewful of worshippers, "was in keeping with the bent of her soul. The deeply lined face, the too marked and massive features, were united with an air of delicate refinement, which in one way was the more impressive, because it seemed to proceed so entirely from within. Nay, the inward beauty would sometimes quite transform the outward harshness; there would be moments when the thin hands which entwined themselves in their eagerness, the earnest figure which bowed forward to speak and hear, the deep gaze moving from one face to another with a grave appeal,—all these seemed the transparent symbols that showed the presence of a wise, benignant soul."

And, this chronicler should have added, she had no humour about herself.

When Lewes died in 1878 she felt like a child abandoned in a thick wood. She who from childhood had so craved affection stood staring into the dark trees which stretched in every direction, and was as abjectly despairing as the widowed Queen Victoria. She was nearly sixty; how could she get along without her literary adviser, soother, letter-writer, package-opener, errand-runner, friend, majordomo—the "beloved husband" of the dedications? Her writing stopped; she said she would never write again.

And then seventeen months later she astonished everybody and shocked some by marrying John Walter Cross, an American banker twenty-five years or so her junior, who had been a friend of the Lewes household for years; and once more life was "intensely interesting" and "a wonderful blessing."

But it was an interlude, a last mirage. The marriage took place in May, and the following December, having contracted a bad cold at a concert, she died

It was raining steadily on Highgate Cemetery. A Unitarian minister in an earnest voice repeated her prayer, "O may I join the choir invisible." The people bowed their heads as she was laid in the same grave as Lewes, and cold wet drops flattened on the wood.

> He first deceas'd—she, for a little tried
> To live without him, liked it not and died.

XVI

ELINOR WYLIE

ELINOR WYLIE

SHELLEY, whom Elinor Wylie all but worshipped, has written in *A Defense of Poetry,*

"Poetry is not like reasoning, a power to be exerted according to the determination of the will . . . for the mind in creation is as a fading coal, which some invisible influence, like an inconstant wind, awakens to transitory brightness. . . ."

One's accomplishment can never go beyond, but in time may equal, one's admirations. "A man's reach must exceed his grasp"—because his grasp can never exceed his reach. Only in the lives of the great are the two commensurate. The career of Elinor Wylie is an interesting comment on this text.

Elinor Morton Hoyt, born in the fall of 1885 in New Jersey, but by blood and allegiance a Pennsylvanian, was the daughter of Roosevelt's solicitor-general. The tall slender girl with a wealth of "tawny chestnut" hair married Philip Hichborn of Washington, and bore a son. But the conventional official life of Washington stifled her; she was blessed and punished with an imagination. More than that, she was going through an extremely unhappy period because of the behavior of her husband and the death of her father. Horace Wylie, a neighbor much older than herself, a husband and the father of five children, seemed, suddenly, to answer a deep need in her for—what was it?—splendour?—

articulate understanding? She has called him the most fascinating conversationalist she ever knew—and surely if any one could judge brilliant talk, she could. Some kind of spiritual compulsion was on them; the nature of it is not clear, but with the essential fineness of Elinor Hoyt as premise, the only possible conclusion is that it seemed, at the time, justified. They walked out of their respective homes and sailed to Europe, and for years, in various and strange countries, wandered together, like the two ghosts in a noble Japanese play who could not find a resting place, for their hearts were troubled.

Though she considered becoming a painter, she abandoned colours for words, and in 1911 her first volume of verse, *Incidental Numbers,* was published privately and anonymously in England: forty-three undistinguished pages between blue-grey boards. But even this volume hints at an unusual person—especially in the sonnet about the devil being a gentleman.

In Washington the young husband had faith that Elinor would return; he would wait. But at last his friends persuaded him that there was nothing for him to do but get a divorce. He shot himself instead. Then Elinor Hichborn married Horace Wylie.

These years were the difficult schooling of Elinor Wylie's heart and character, and therefore of her poetry.

After a time she returned to the United States, and was divorced from the fascinating conversationalist, and arranged the exquisite pieces of delicate glassware, which she loved, in a New York apartment; and in 1921 *Nets to Catch the Wind* was published, and the poet acclaimed.

What had the weaving of Horace Wylie's words done for her mind? The son whose growing up she had not witnessed? The children who died? England? Sicily?

> Say not of beauty she is good,
> Or aught but beautiful . . .

This, in her wanderings, she had learned, and was never to unlearn, though she was to change as her experience changed. "The heart's intention," she noted in her last volume, is to "be both brave and good." But the day of her death I think she might have reiterated, "Say not of beauty she is good, or aught but beautiful." Only, she would have understood more explicitly that beauty of conduct, which is goodness, is a part of all beauty, being its flower.

Nets to Catch the Wind reveals a proud and fastidious woman, struggling against the world and herself, and at intervals coming out into a clear quiet space. Yeats has said that "we make out of the quarrel with others, rhetoric, but of the quarrel with ourselves, poetry." When she cries, Live like the eagle, live like the mole, she is soliciting and preparing for the lonely and sacred wisdom. But within were deterrents; without were enemies: the cold hard surfaces she affected, the gleaming metals, the petrified flowers: "drops . . . like bells of glass," "black onyx cherries," "silver wasp-nests." She is often too clever in this first signed book, and her bravery is sometimes rigid, like a posture. She is not suspicious, yet, of her own facility.

But in *Black Armour,* published two years later, she has less patience with the illusory and false.

> My body is weary to death of my mischievous brain:
> I am weary forever and ever of being brave.

She takes stock of her virtues and faults: which is an early stage of spiritual evolution.

> I was, being human, born alone;
> I am, being woman, hard beset;
> I live by squeezing from a stone
> The little nourishment I get.
>
> In masks outrageous and austere
> The years go by in single file;
> But none has merited my fear
> And none has quite escaped my smile.

This is alive, and simple, and warm. But she reverts to the virtuoso lady of dexterous, dazzling technique. She has a long way to go to meet Shelley whom she admires.

Some gave her flattery, for she called it praise; but some with their whole hearts believed in her. William Rose Benét, poet in his own right, who had been a close friend of her brother, remarked in a questionaire, when she was still little-known, that she was his "favourite poet." He admired her poetry for itself, but he also fell in love with "that ghostly rose that was her face," and all it signified.

In 1924 the high-strung fragile woman married the discerning, kind, stanch man. In the summertime, at the MacDowell Colony for artists at Peterborough, New Hampshire, they walked arm-in-arm in the cool of the evening. She was extremely nervous, and sometimes difficult, but she was lovely. One night, on the front stoop of the Main House, while a few of the colonists were discussing the different things poets have likened the moon to, she stared at a ravage of illumined cloud. "But only one poet," she murmured, "has made the perfect comparison." As they waited for her to tell them which poet she referred to, she looked slight and frangible in the veiling dusk, her thin boyishly-square shoulders inclined, her delicate hands lacing and unlacing, her long beautiful shadow of a throat lifted. Softly she quoted Shelley, and each word, before it was loosed upon the stillness, was lovingly formed by her mouth:

> And like a dying lady, lean and pale,
> Who totters forth, wrapp'd in a gauzy veil,
> Out of her chamber, led by the insane
> And feeble wanderings of her fading brain,
> The moon arose up in the murky east
> A white and shapeless mass.

Did she feel homesick that summer twilight, and during the years which followed, for the fervent world of "mad Shelley"? For a while she wrote fewer poems, being engrossed with prose: *Jennifer Lorn,* sub-titled "A Sedate Extravaganza," *The Venetian Glass Nephew,* in which she went further in elaborate and fond artifice, and then—as tribute to her master— *The Orphan Angel,* an apocryphal rescue of Shelley from the Mediterranean and his fortunes in a fabulous America. Her prose became less mannered; but though, in certain traits of temperament and in some of the incidents of her life, Shelley's counterpart, she was not at this time equal in purity of poetical outlook to the visionary and impractical young man who floated emancipating tracts in bottles. She was in the habit of prose, and began another novel, *Mr. Hodge and Mr. Hazard,* which she liked best of all her novels. Nevertheless her true country was poetry and she longed to return.

Trivial Breath (1928), her third volume of poetry, marked a transition. At last she had learned what to shun, but not quite how to shun it.

> Go study to disdain
> The frail, the overfine,
> That tapers to a line
> Knotted about the brain.

In these poems which derive in part from literature, she does not falsify life, for she knows that it is "useless to pretend." She had contrived her exquisiteness as a person digs a ditch, and if she had not been careful, might have fallen into it. But she was not stumbling, she was walking straight. Perhaps she re-read the four poems called "A Red Carpet for Shelley," and disapproved of the too familiar "my dear." No, they were not good enough; they seemed artificial. The flower of her early work was not blooming as gorgeously as might have been expected. But she must have taken comfort from knowing, what she must have known, that there would be a magnificent stand next season. In *Trivial Breath* was the promise: the quiet "Confession of Faith," the sure "Last Supper," "revelation at its lips."

At Peterborough in 1925 she had predicted, in a tempestuous and fanatic-sounding but really prophetic moment, her death in about three years. She was not frightened. In spite of some appearances to the contrary, she had always insisted that she was temperamentally Puritan.

> Down to the Puritan marrow of my bones
> There's something in this richness which I hate.

And she had loved

> Bare hills, cold silver on a sky of slate,
> A thread of water, churned to milky spate
> Streaming through slanted pastures fenced with stones . . .

She looked, with the stern favour of one committed to the austerities, upon death, as upon one more reticence of art.

Vanity she had lost, who had seemed at times conscious of her least movement; who had described herself often, as in "Preferences":

> These to me are beautiful people;
> Thick hair sliding in a ripple;
> A tall throat, round as a column;
> A mournful mouth, small and solemn,
> Having to confound the mourner
> Irony in either corner;
> The limbs fine, narrow and strong;
> Like the wind they walk along,
> Like the whirlwind, bad to follow;
> The cheekbones high, the cheeks hollow,
> The eyes large and wide apart,
> They carry a dagger in the heart
> So keen and clean it never rankles. . . .
> They wear small bones in wrists and ankles.

Of course, in soft-clashing mauve taffeta at once smart and elegant, or in neat cool black and white voile, or daintily carrying a little bright parasol down the maple-shaded road at Peterborough, or at any other time, or place, she could have been easily excused for being preoccupied with herself, for who was more charming? And she was never wholly preoccupied with herself, nor preoccupied in a small way. A highlight of humour had always livened and relieved the gravity of her hazel eyes, and she had always been capable of delightful fooling, as in "Parting Gift,"

> I cannot give you the Metropolitan Tower,
> I cannot give you heaven;
> Not the nine Visigoth crowns in the Cluny Museum;
> Nor happiness, even.
> But I can give you a very small purse
> Made out of field-mouse skin,
> With a painted picture of the universe
> And seven blue tears within.

But when she came to write *Angels and Earthly Creatures*, though there was more reason for it, she was no longer proud, except in the fine necessary sense. She claimed no humility: she felt it.

Sainte-Beuve has said that "style is the only thing that is immortal in literature." When Elinor Wylie departed for England in the summer of 1928 her style was a perfected instrument; the medium had been subdued and mastered. Echoes of Greek and Latin lyricists, of the early anonymous balladists, of the Jacobean metaphysicians, and particularly of Donne, were heard no more. She had come to believe something similar to what Keats wrote Taylor, and what she could not have accepted when she first started to write: that "poetry should surprise by a fine excess, and not by singularity." "Excess" would not have been her word; perhaps "fulness." She no longer wished to astonish and arrest by erratic phrases, intricate rhyming, and brilliant but sometimes shallow, merely flashing wit. Yeats has called fancy amusement and imagination revelation. This distinction must have had a new clarity for her now. The purification of her style had been concomitant to a growth in character and mind. The hard shiny early style had been a defense; the glowing human later style was as different as flesh from metal (though incandescent), and was an avowal that spiritually she had passed beyond the need of defense.

In England she was under "an invisible influence." All her previous poetry had been but an earnest and foreshadowing of this "high breeding in words and argument." The personality had expanded and become integrated. A true aristocrat, she did not apologize to nor compromise with what Cervantes has called "that ancient law-giver, the vulgar." Now, as in her previous writing, she was drawn by "the fascination of what's difficult"—but with a difference, and with a new emphasis. Style was not separated from meaning, but fused with it. Death, or the premonition of death, fuses all. "So short a time remains . . ." "In this last minute and no more . . ." She was perfectly serene, who had been often agitated. "Today it is eternity I ask . . ."

Then one afternoon in England she fell down a staircase and seriously injured her spine.

It was not a long flight of steps but the turn was polished smooth by age, and it is not strange that a light-footed person, descending quickly to speak to her hostess, slipped and plunged. She got up and walked into the garden and, scarcely referring to the pain in her back, sat through tea on the lawn and dinner, and the next morning boarded a train alone. The doctor summoned to her London flat discovered by X-ray that the sacrum of the spine was fractured. She did not write her husband about the accident, lest he worry. When he joined her later she was out of bed again and moving around, and no onlooker could have guessed that the hurt would prove in a few months, when the consequences had had time to work themselves out, mortal.

But a noble leave-taking had already been written, "Hymn to Earth":

Farewell, incomparable element
Whence man arose, where he shall not return;

  . . . .

Hail, element of earth, receive thy own,
And cherish, at thy charitable breast,
This man, this mongrel beast:
He ploughs the sand, and, at his hardest need,
He sows himself for seed;

  . . . .

Receive him as thy lover for an hour
Who will not weary, by a longer stay,
The kind embrace of clay;
Even within thine arms he is dispersed

To nothing, as at first;
The air flings downward from its four-quartered tower
Him whom the flames devour;
At the full tide, at the flood,
The sea is mingled with his salty blood:
The traveller dust, although the dust be vile,
Sleeps as thy lover for a little while.

And in manuscript was a sequence of love sonnets so spontaneous, so patrician, so clear and impassioned and calm, that they can be compared only to the finest love sonnets, Christina Rossetti's, and Keats', and those of Shakespeare himself.

In the first of the nineteen, one hears the majestic and great accent, as she affirms the dignity of the human soul, caught in a mesh of time:

> Although these words are false, none shall prevail
> To prove them in translation less than true
> Or overthrow their dignity, or undo
> The faith implicit in a fabulous tale;
> The ashes of this error shall exhale
> Essential verity, and two by two
> Lovers devout and loyal shall renew
> The legend, and refuse to let it fail.

She came home to America sick in body, but it has been said that never had she been so beautiful. Now, without knowing it, she described her own face:

> Its symmetry is perfect and severe
> Because the barbarous force of agonies
> Broke it, and mended it, and made it clear.

232

On December 15, 1928, she selected and arranged *Angels and Earthly Creatures;* and the next day, exactly three and a half years after her Peterborough prophecy, died.

Beauty had reached, for her, its fullest connotation. It was the proper time to die. After being for three volumes not more than a gifted poet, she had suddenly with her last volume become what, even before time has clarified and given perspective, one is tempted to call a great poet. Certainly, before death she had joined those "of the most delicate sensibility and the most enlarged imagination . . . at war with every base desire"; and in death could say with Shelley:

"Poetry arises from within, like the colour of a flower which fades and changes as it is developed, and the conscious portions of our natures are unprophetic either of its approach or its departure. . . It arrests the vanishing apparitions which haunt the interlunations of life and . . . redeems from decay the visitations of the divinity in man . . ."

It is peculiarly fitting that her mortal body should not have survived her induction into immortal art.

XVII

KATHERINE MANSFIELD

I HAVE been wondering, as I studied the life of Katherine Mansfield, if it is a spiritual principle that what the souls longs to be, it becomes.

A photograph of her, taken in 1914 when she was twenty-six, is the face of the usual pretty young woman: dewy dark eyes, tilted nose, easy mouth, a bloom-like complexion, unlined. Strikingly different is a picture taken eight years later when, at thirty-four, she stood on the brink of death. The face is thinner, with shadows in the hollows; the mouth firmer, being versed in pain; the hair is arranged more simply; the earrings have been discarded; the eyes are larger, they seem to pierce through space, and see beyond.

Her letters, if traced from year to year, reveal a similar change. In 1914 they are sometimes a little flippant, or warped by violence, or trivial, as when she says she is not going to get drunk any more, or faintly off pitch—false; though, even then, they seem to wish for something more important. Then for eight years the letters become increasingly sensitive and true. It is as if, on a shadowed hill, the clouds began to disperse and the light parted. Her last autumn, in 1922, she is glass of crystal; she is simple, "as one would be simple before God." In 1915, when healthy, she had written, "All will be well." In 1922, about to die, she wrote triumphantly, "All is well."

It would seem that what her soul had longed to be it had unerringly become, and that illness had hastened the process. Tuberculosis did not make her the finest English short story writer. It could not do that. But in health the same spiritual development might have required five, ten, fifteen years longer. Illness was the danger which startled her from lethargy into swiftness. She wrote, the year tuberculosis was diagnosed, that

"my present state of health is a great gain. It makes things so rich, so important, so longed for . . . changes one's focus. When one is little and ill and far away in a remote bedroom beyond is marvellous. . ."

The day she first coughed blood she wrote her husband that

"since this little attack I've had, a queer thing has happened. My love and longing for the external world . . . has suddenly increased a million times. When I think of the little flowers that grow in grass, and little streams and places where we can lie and look up at the clouds—Oh, I simply ache for them . . ."

And she wrote, with a discernment born of her own malady, of her doctor on the Riviera,

"He has the disease himself. I *recognized* his smile—just the least shade too bright—and his strange joyousness as he came to meet me . . . the gleam—the faint glitter on the plant that the frost has laid a finger on . . ."

Katherine Mansfield, whose real name was Kathleen

Beauchamp, was born in 1888 in Kaori near Wellington, New Zealand, third daughter in a family of five.
The Beauchamps, who had been residents of New Zealand for three generations, lived in a large white house
with a narrow pillared veranda, far back from the road.
A garden sloped in terraces down to a stone wall
smothered in nasturtiums, which had three gates, the
Visitors', the Tradesmen's, and an enormous old iron
pair which "clashed and clamoured" when the little girl
and her brother swung back and forth on them, merrily.
The mother was charming and impractical, the father
stern and English. The maternal grandmother was nice
to sleep with, and made good jelly.

At thirteen, as was proper, Kathleen took the long
sea journey to England, and was enrolled at Queen's
College, Harley Street, London. But she was less
intrigued by her surroundings than by people; less interested in studies than in amusing herself with the
world. It was typical of her that one day when the
old Principal who taught Bible History asked any
young lady who had been chased by a wild bull to
hold up her hand, Kathleen, seeing no other, waved
hers frantically.

When she went home at eighteen, she did not appreciate the fresh quality of a far green island set in the
sea, and wished herself gone. On a camping trip through
the bush, she spent a lot of time wondering what this
power was, that moved in her, whimsical and deep as

wind; and which she should become, a musician or a writer. She was a proficient violoncellist and loved to play her instrument, but decided that she would rather be a writer. So, at twenty, with a small allowance from Father in her pocket, and excited, she turned her face a second time toward England.

But recognition did not come as quickly as the youthful heart had dreamed it. Her stories were regularly rejected, and the only parts she could get in travelling opera companies and the cinema were small. But when, after a minor illness, she was convalescent in Bavaria, she wrote a series of satires for *The New Age,* which were collected for *In a German Pension,* and went into three editions. The publisher fell into bankruptcy and her earnings stopped at fifteen pounds advance royalties. That seemed a lot of money.

Then one day at the home of W. L. George the novelist she met an Oxford undergraduate, tall, with a long nose, slanting forehead, dark hair, and eyes in which she read her destiny. For this John Middleton Murry she began to contribute stories to *Rhythm,* his hopeful literary venture, and when it failed, to its successor, *The Blue Review,* and when it also was defunct, to *The Signature.* In the course of all this collaboration, they were married.

One need not try to follow the pretty young woman and her new husband to the red brick cottage at Cholesbury, Buckinghamshire, for the door is closed. But only three years before, she had gone for a walk in dripping wet woods, barefoot—and one surmises she was still impetuous. Underfoot there was soft silk grass, and there were sharp twigs, and pebbles. . . . Later, they were in Paris, counting and recounting francs; and then in a draughty cottage at Great Missenden; then in a small house with steep steps, in St. John's Wood, London, where her brother "Chummie" visited her for a week before setting off for the war and getting killed. She went alone to Bandol on the French Riviera, trying in self-preservation not to remember, and trying desperately to remember every detail, for now only New Zealand days, with the happy dead boy, seemed to matter at all.

The war put a deep mark, like a brand, on Katherine Mansfield's impressionable mind. She staggered under the blow, and never completely recovered from the dizzy concussion.

In after years she recalled how she and her brother walked up and down Acacia Road, in the gathering dusk, the last time she saw him. From an old fruit tree a pear dropped, "hard as a stone."

"Did you hear that, Katie? Can you find it? By Jove—that familiar sound."

Their hands move over the thin moist grass. He picks it up, and unconsciously, as of old, polishes it on his handkerchief.

"Do you remember the enormous number of pears there used to be on that old tree?"

"Down by the violet bed."

"And how after there'd been a Southerly Buster we used to go out with clothes baskets to pick them up?"

Back and forth, back and forth they paced, calling up their childhood; and in tenderness promised each other to return to New Zealand some day, together. And he passed his arm around her, and the air smelled chill and heavy.

"It's curious—my absolute confidence that I'll come back. I feel it's as certain as this pear."

"I feel that too."

"I couldn't not come back. You know that feeling. It's awfully mysterious."

The shadows on the grass are long and strange; a puff of strange wind whispers in the ivy and the cold moon touches them with silver.

She shivers.

"You're cold."

"Dreadfully cold."

He puts his arm around her. Suddenly he kisses her—

"Good-bye, darling."

"Ah, why do you say that!"

"Darling, good-bye . . . good-bye."

Nothing stays quite so long as that which goes, and six years after, she wrote to a friend:

"Ah, Brett, I hope with all my heart that you have not known anyone who has died young—long before their time. It is bitterness."

"Six Years After"—it is the title of one of her best

stories, in which the mother of a dead son on a moving ship stares out over a pallid expanse of water.

This is anguish! How is it to be borne? Still, it is not the idea of her suffering which is unbearable—it is his. Can one do nothing for the dead? And for a long time the answer had been—Nothing!

Captain Leslie Heron Beauchamp had died in France, and when would she die, and where? She began to be a little morbid. "At times the fear of death," she wrote in her *Journal,* "is dreadful." She had had arthritis, and then had caught a cold; and the cold had gone into pleurisy, and now she had tuberculosis. One night she dreamed that suddenly her whole body was breaking up into pieces.

"A long terrible shiver, you understand—the spinal column and the bones and every bit and particle quaking. It sounded in my ears a low, confused din, and there was a sense of floating greenish brilliance, like broken glass. . . ."

And then physical fear gave way before a spiritual concern.

"Oh, Life! accept me—make me worthy—teach me. I write that. I look up. The leaves move in the garden, the sky is pale, and I catch myself weeping. It is hard—it is hard to make a good death. . . ."

From this time on, she exacted more and more from her writing; and all that she had written previously seemed to her of no account.

"You see, it's too late to beat about the bush any longer. They are cutting down the cherry trees; the orchard is sold—"

She would not consent to a re-issue of *In a German Pension,* which had been well received, because it seemed to her inferior. She was writing "The Daughters of the Late Colonel" at top speed, lest she die before it was finished and sent off. She wrote her husband,

"A great deal is copied and carefully addressed to you, in case any misfortune should happen to me. Cheerful! But there is a great black bird flying over me, and I am so frightened it will settle—so terrified. I don't know exactly what *kind* he is."

But years went by, and though she still lived, many changes had taken place. Where were the snows of yesteryear?—and where were Anne Estelle Rice, who had laughed on the beach at Looe; and Lady Ottoline Morrell, who had smiled when she had spoken, in wartime, of the corruption of the world; and Virginia Woolf who "had the same job" and was "after so very much the same thing"; and D. H. Lawrence, with whom she had shared a whole spring full of bluebells; and the Honourable Dorothy Brett, painter, whom she had felt close to, being so much the accurate passionate painter herself; and her cousin, Countess Russell, the author "Elizabeth," who had described, as they lay on a bed, "a certain very exquisite *Rose,* single, pale yellow with coral tipped petals"; and L. M., helpful in a crisis, but irritating; and all the likeable servants in *pensions* and hotels: Juliette at Bandol, "like double stock, tufty, strong, very sweet, very gay," and Mrs. Honey the ancient Cornish woman, nimble and small, with a fresh skin ("There do be a *handsome* bath for eë"), and Marie, who had said once that bananas gave the fruit dish "effect"; and Tomlinson; and de la Mare; and Gerhardi; and Koteliansky in his big black hat, who had translated her beloved Tchekhov...? She saw scarcely anyone now, and sometimes she was lonely.

"People are vile," she would exclaim, and almost the next moment, "Oh the beauty of the human soul—the Beauty of it—" and she realized, disheartened, that those two attitudes must be reconciled. Only toward the end of her life, when she had gone to Gurdjieff's Institute at Fontainebleau, to try to get well, did she decide, without any possibility of changing her mind and going back on it, that

"after all, there are the seeds of what we long after in everybody and if one remembers that, any surroundings are . . . possible, at least."

There is no doubt, from the evidence of her *Journal,* and expurgated letters, and friends, that her relation with her husband contributed, in some measure, to her confusion. She loved him, she says, "in the old—in the ancient way, through and through," but during the estrangement of her last year she cried,

"What remains of all those years together? . . . Who *gave up* and *why*?"

She was convinced, now, that to cure the body one must cure the mind, or soul, and believed the Gurdjieff Institute the right medicine for both; but she held back—why?

"Fear," she answers. "Fear of what? Doesn't it come down to fear of losing J—? . . . But, good Heavens! Face things. What have you of him now? . . . You are important to him as a dream. Not as a living reality. For you are not one. . . . Yet there is a deep, sweet, tender flooding of feeling in my heart which is love for him and longing for him. But what is the good of it as things stand? Life together, with me ill, is simply torture with happy moments."

They had love of literature in common, and memories, and the mind's respect; they read Jane Austen together, and Goethe's *Conversations with Eckermann,* and Dickens, and Chaucer, and Congreve; they showed each other the wild flowers they found, and the sea in altering light; they played a special game of their own, shieing stones at a rock; they shared the pleasure of music, and picked mushrooms, and swooped forward, together, in a Swiss sleigh, over the silent and mysterious snow. "We could not, knowing what we know," she said, "belong to others who know not."

But there was the question of belonging to one's self; and in France, Cornwall, Italy, Switzerland—wherever she went—though she longed for him to follow, when he arrived, was there not a falling movement of disappointment? Only in solitude could she experience "the luxury of not having to explain." And in her final mood of extreme honesty with herself, several years after what had been planned as a splendid reunion at Isola Bella, she said sadly,

"I think of the garden at Isola, Bella and the furry bees and the house-wall so warm. But then I remember what we really felt there—the blanks, the silences, the anguish of continual misunderstanding."

No, the conjugal relation was, to her, not simple, and not serene—whether from her illness entirely, or from other causes too. Let us be just. To be ill is not easy, nor to be near illness, sometimes, listening to it cough, ministering to it, and curbing one's healthy instincts. Yet, after nine years of marriage, she could say,

"It seems to me the only possible relation that really is satisfying. . . . To know *one other* seems to me a far greater adventure than to be on kissing acquaintance with dear knows how many. It takes a lifetime and it's far more 'wonderful' as time goes on."

But what of Koteliansky—"Kot"? Two years after her marriage she had written one of her infrequent letters to this Russian, ending,

"Write me *often often,* for I shall be very lonely, I know. Good-bye, just for now. I press your hands *tightly*—Goodbye."

Koteliansky visited the Murrys often, and spent one whole Christmas with them, at Hampstead; and he and Katherine discussed Tchekhov, with joy, and she helped him translate Tchekhov's letters into English. His judgment she esteemed, and his friendship she valued. One of her letters to him begins, casually, by mentioning a bit of cracked ivory on his desk, and the pictures in his room, and sights, and smells, those little things which are remembered only under emotional stress: rain, and half-light, and people running downstairs, and a heavy door slamming, and umbrellas spreading black in the street, which was darker now, suddenly; and she breaks off, "Dear friend—do not think evil of me— forgive me."

And at another time she wrote,

"Not a day passes but I think of you . . . It is *good* love— not the erotic bad kind."

The last year, they talked about individuality, and being strong and single, because, it appears, he was the person she could discuss these vital things with most profitably. When she determined on Fontainebleau, she wrote him first about her "private revolution." With him she strove passionately to be honest, and when he criticized, she was humble.

But humility toward the rest of the world came painfully and slowly:

"I wonder why," she wrote in her *Journal,* "it should be so very difficult to be humble. . . Calm yourself. Clear yourself. . . Anything I write in this mood will be no good; it will be full of *sediment*. One must learn, one must practice, to *forget* oneself. I can't tell the truth about Aunt Anne unless I am free to look into her life without self-consciousness."

In a German Pension had been the brilliant cynicism of twenty-three; then for six years she had lost her great fluency. *Prelude,* a blue paper book issued by the Hogarth Press, had announced that she coveted a fuller and more difficult power; in Paris during the terrible bombardment with her illness aggravated and her mind depressed, she had written three short stories which were accepted. Then her husband had become editor of the *Athenaeum,* and at last she had found an outlet, and for over a year had written penetrating criticisms of current books, the trend of which she found "quite without any value whatsoever"; then in the spring of 1920 *Bliss* had appeared, and been mildly praised; and at Ospedaletti in Italy, and Mentone in Southern France, and Montana in Switzerland, she had coughed and coughed, and gone on valiantly with her self-perfecting. It was *The Garden Party,* in 1922, which confirmed her right to stand beside Tchekhov: with the title story, and "At the Bay," and "The Young Girl," and "Life of Ma Parker," and "Her First Ball," and "The Singing Lesson," and "The Stranger," and "An Ideal Family." . . . But she told Koteliansky when she went to Gurdjieff's,

"I do not want to write any more stories until I am a less terribly poor human being";

and she told her husband,

"I want to write, but differently—far more steadily . . . The old mechanism isn't mine any longer and I can't control the new."

What would she have written if she had lived? A play such as she once spoke of? No story in *The Young Girl,* published posthumously, compares with any story in *The Garden Party;* and no story in *The Dove's Nest,* except "The Doll's House" and "Six Years After." But they are the work she had chosen not to publish; and, like her mild poetry, though they have not increased her influence on present-day writing in England and America, they have not diminished it.

At Gurdjieff's Institute she had, as substitutes for Rib her dog and Wingley her cat, chickens, and cows, and pigs all around her. It was not the home she had dreamed of "with J—for a husband and a little boy for a son," but in many ways it seemed larger and more significant. Here were the values of Tchekhov and Dostoevsky; for the Institute had been founded on the faith that (in the words of Mrs. Frank Lloyd Wright)

"interior life—through self-control, through non-identification with the ever-changing states of one's being, through sacrifices, through never-tiring efforts to understand more and do more, through willingness to suffer more when needed —could be made real, could be made even immortal."

In 1918 Katherine Mansfield had said, "I cannot believe in immortality." But now she declared, "Anxiety I never feel." She saw that aesthetics and ethics cannot be separated: to be a better writer she must be a better woman. Trying to put her beliefs into practice made her wonderfully happy. According to a friend who saw her at this time,

"she looked at all and at each with sharp, intense, dark eyes that burned with hunger for impressions."

Though too ill to eat in the hall, or do odd jobs in the gardens and kitchen, with the others, she took part imaginatively: she was not separate. The time of tempers had passed, and of melancholy fits of weeping. Now she felt for the whole world, instead of just for Koteliansky, "*good* love, not the erotic bad kind."

"Really," she said, "I have not felt so well in years. What had disturbed me lately was that I felt as though it was all to be denied me—the very life, I mean, which I want to live. But here today I feel that I can build up a life within me which death will not destroy."

One day she was allowed to feed corn to the chickens, and when they rushed to her flapping their numerous wings she cried in a childlike transport, "Oh this is wonderful! I feel terribly important!"

After three months of this life she invited her husband to visit her for a few days; and for him, when he was expected, combed the dark bangs down again over the white white forehead. She was eager to tell him about the book she meant to write, and to show him how far, in spiritual development, she had gone. . . .

Death threw bright beams behind and ahead, illuminating all. That day, in the deeps of her consciousness, she must have heard the echo of her voice saying, as personal prophecy, in 1918,

"I am quite certain that it is all wrong to live isolated and shut away—There ought to be something fine and gay that we toss about among us, and never let fall—*a spirit* . . ."

And three years later, in gratitude for trouble,

"Bodily suffering . . . has changed for ever everything—even the *appearance* of the world is not the same—there is something added. Everything has its shadow. Is it right to resist much suffering? Do you know, I feel it has been an immense privilege. . . ."

And then, when she had begun the long fight of the soul,

"One must be true to one's vision of life—in every single particular . . . The only thing to do is to try from tonight to be stronger and better—to be whole."

And, only this year, when severely tested,

"All I know really, really, is that though one thing after another has been taken from me, I am not annihilated, and that I hope—more than hope—believe."

And to Dorothy Brett, recently,

"Life is a mystery. . . But who shall say where death ends and resurrection begins. That's what one must do. Give it, the idea of *resurrection,* the power that death would like to have. Be born again and born again faster than we die . . ."

She must have looked, that day, "like one who wins, and not like one who loses."

John Middleton Murry arrived early in the afternoon of January 9, 1923, and they had tea together, and talked. As they left the study-house, a friend wanted to fetch Katherine an umbrella, but she said, "Oh no, I love the rain tonight, I want the feeling of it on my face. . ."

At ten o'clock, as she reached the top of the stairs, she had a terrible coughing spell and haemorrhage. She had said that the known was only a mere shadow, that the unknown was the real and substantial. By ten-thirty she had gone to find out.

THE END